HOSTAGE IN IRAQ

In the remembrance of God:
For without doubt in the remembrance
of God do hearts find rest.

(Qur'an 13.28)

A gift to the author by the artist Vaseem Mohammed

HOSTAGE
IN
IRAQ

NORMAN KEMBER

DARTON·LONGMAN+TODD

First published in 2007 by
Darton, Longman and Todd Ltd
1 Spencer Court
140–142 Wandsworth High Street
London SW18 4JJ

ISBN-10 0-232-52699-0
ISBN-13 978-0-232-52699-8

A catalogue record for this book is available
from the British Library.

www.normankember.org

Designed and produced by Sandie Boccacci
Set in 12/14½pt Bembo
Printed and bound in Great Britain by
The Cromwell Press, Trowbridge, Wiltshire

To all those who supported my wife, Pat,
during those distressing months.

A VULNERABLE MAN

A Song for Norman

He's far from being a young man, his muscles are
    not strong,
so call him old and frail then – you won't be too
    far wrong.
But there's a spirit in him that's sane and strong
    and sure:
the muscle or the spirit – say, which should count
    for more?
When all our wealth and weapons have done the
    most they can,
how will they measure up to a vulnerable man?

The young men in their thousands, with weapons
    in their hands,
they're burning to bring freedom to those in
    foreign lands.
But there's a weakness in them that cripples each
    brave deed:
they're trained and honed for battle – it's peace
    that people need.
When all their wealth and weapons have done
    the most they can,
they still can't measure up to a vulnerable man.

The weary, battered people, worn out with strife
    and pain,
are desperately seeking to live their lives again.

But do they need the young men with death at
    their command,
or someone with a sharp wit and eyes that
    understand?
When all their wealth and weapons have done
    the most they can,
the people need the soul of a vulnerable man.

You leaders and you fighters, when will you
    comprehend
that any fool can break things – a wise man learns
    to mend?
And Jesus knew the answer, and Gandhi knew it
    too,
and still it lies, deep down, in the likes of me and
    you.
When all our wealth and weapons have done the
    most they can,
we still won't have the power of a vulnerable
    man:
yes, when all our wealth and weapons have done
    the most they can,
we find we need the soul of a vulnerable man.

SUE GILMURRAY
The Anglican Pacifist Fellowship
31 March 2006

CONTENTS

INTRODUCTION

This book is a personal account of my experiences as a delegate with the Christian Peacemaker Teams to Iraq in November 2005 and my days spent as a kidnap victim until March 2006. The bulk of the writing is based on my memory and I take responsibility for any errors. As an *aide-mémoire*, I have the transcript of my debriefing to the police which was made within a month of arriving back in England.

Other sources include three accounts that I wrote in Baghdad on the CPT computer before the kidnap and some of the writing from my 'captivity notebook'. Unfortunately the original notebook in which I described our experiences in Jordan and Baghdad at the beginning of our trip was taken by our captors, as was my camera with some of my photographs of Baghdad.

James Loney wrote extensive notes about our captivity in his notebook, and I hope that he will write a more accurate account of our experiences than you will read here. I have referred to his outline of events to check some dates and for information concerning the series of fictions we were told by our captors about release.

In the section on events at home during our captivity, I have relied on the sources which I have acknowledged in that chapter. The minister of my church, the Revd Robert Gardiner, contributed substantially and I have also consulted with family and my many friends in Christian peace organisations. I have not given credit to the full cast of supporters. For this I apologise.

By starting to give some account of the intense media interest in our homecoming I quickly discovered that a whole book could be written about those frantic few days. I have only provided a brief summary.

There do not appear to be standard transliterations of the sounds of Arabic words into the western alphabet. Here we have tried to be consistent.

There are so many people who should be thanked – first and foremost, my wife Pat, who paid so dearly for accepting my decision to go to Iraq, then Jim and Harmeet for putting up with me so patiently over those three-and-a-half months. There are a host of people, many of them unknown to me personally, who supported my wife with visits, letters, cards and flowers. A number of others who played a part in the story are written into the text and I hope will accept that mention as a 'thank you'.

I am grateful to Teresa de Bertodano who oversaw my attempts to transform a scientific report into a literary account without losing my 'voice', and all the members of the DLT team who worked so enthusiastically to bring this book to publication.

1

KIDNAP

Saturday 26 November

The van door closes and we are kidnapped. Just
like that, with the precision of a general's finger
snap. *James Loney*

We plunged into a Baghdad souk, a wonderful confusion of
all manner of goods and humanity. Drive down a wide road
and suddenly you are in it – barrows loaded with old clothes,
new clothes (all sizes, all ages, both sexes), carpets, curtains,
bales of material. Our driver eased the car through the crowds
and people reluctantly stepped aside.

Our people carrier came to rest in the hardware section –
sanitary ware, paints, tiles, furniture, a man carving a door,
motor parts (I saw a bath used to test tyres for leaks), lights,
electrical goods. Leaving the driver in the vehicle, five of us
continued on foot; the interpreter, myself and the other two
members of the Christian Peacemaker Teams delegation; our
leader, James Loney, coordinator of CPT in Canada, and
Harmeet Singh Sooden, an engineer in his early thirties, also
a Canadian citizen. The final member of the group was an
American, Tom Fox of the resident CPT Team in Baghdad.

Harmeet Singh Sooden (above, left), *Tom Fox* (above, right) *and James Loney* (left)

We worked our way back to the main souk, and as our tall interpreter strode to our destination we struggled to keep up with him, fearful of getting lost as we squeezed past stalls and stallholders and on into the square in front of the Kadhimain Mosque, the Shia mosque. To the left was a cave-like complex of jewellers' shops; to the right were fruit stalls. On we went down an ancient narrow passage which led to the house of the Shia Imam.

We three delegates had a morning appointment with the Imam, Sayyid Ali, and Tom Fox was accompanying us. The Imam's house had two well-armed guards outside and we had to wait twenty minutes for our appointment. This time we spent talking to the guards about their work in Baghdad – one of them had a working knowledge of English. I also explored the dingy alleyways immediately around the house and took a few photographs of the overhanging wooden galleries.

Eventually we were invited into the house and entered a carpeted anteroom where people were sitting on the floor. I eased myself down, remembering to tuck my feet well in (in the Middle East it is considered the height of bad manners to point the soles of the feet at another). Stage three took us into the presence of a frail man dressed in black – the Imam. This time there were seats around the walls. We were offered tea in small glasses, into which sugar was spooned to about one third of the volume and then the liquid poured on top.

Our interpreter expressed our thanks for the audience. We put questions through him and began to ask about the present situation in Iraq. Hardly had we begun when the door opened and another man appeared. He was apparently a political advisor and, speaking English, took over the meeting. He launched into a long political speech. I took brief records but my notebook disappeared in the kidnap and I fear that the man's tirade was so important that I have no memory of it! He appeared to blame the Sunnis for everything (Shias and Sunnis trace the divisions between them back 1,400 years to the succession from the Prophet Muhammad). From time to time a third man would sidle into the room and present a note or a document. The Imam would sign, return the document and the man would disappear through a door behind the Imam's seat. We learned later that the documents were marriage licences. After an hour and half's tirade we managed to get away. We left via the ancient narrow passage and worked our way back through the souk to the parked vehicle and our driver.

The original idea had been to return to the CPT residence where Greg Rollins, another member of the resident team, was to exchange places with Tom Fox, with perhaps a change of interpreter. The Shia Imam's political advisor had gone on for so long it was decided that we would go straight on to the Sunni mosque, keeping Tom with us. That decision was lethally fateful for Tom but saved Greg from kidnap.

We bought food and drink: vegetable filled wraps and bottles of – was it Seven Up? – which we consumed in the car. We then drove out of the souk area and away towards the Sunni mosque, on the north-west outskirts of Baghdad. We passed the new (a football stadium) and the old (flocks of scruffy sheep herded into stockades in the central reservations of dual carriageways).

The Sunni mosque we were heading for is partially surrounded by a moat. It is a large modern building with tall minarets and a blue tiled dome, and occupies an immense plot of land. It is variously called Um al Ma'ariq (Mother of all battles) or Um al Qurra (Mother of all villages, another name for Mecca) and was completed by the turn of the millennium by Saddam Hussein as the 'grand state mosque', in honour of the first Gulf War in 1991. Four of the towers are based on Kalashnikovs, while another four are based on Scud missiles.

The mosque is now the headquarters of the Sunni Muslim Scholars' Association and members of the Christian Peacemaker Teams had visited the Association without difficulty on several previous occasions.

We drove through a security booth, left car and driver in

The Sunni mosque, Um al Ma'ariq, with its blue tiled roof
(reproduced by permission of Mark Juegensmeyer)

the extensive car park and went in search of the toilets located under the long ramp leading up to the mosque. A walk around to the right of the mosque brought us to a second security booth manned by guards. These ones took our cameras and checked our credentials. Surly in manner, the expressions on their faces were anything but welcoming! We walked past an ornamental pool in the shape of Arab lands and into a two-storey building. We entered an office in which two men were sitting. The one on the left looked like a clerk.

At the far end sat Sunni scholar Ahmed Zaki Al Qasy. We took seats along the right wall and began to question him through our interpreter. I do not have my original notes and cannot recall from memory the substance of the 20–30 minute conversation. It is likely that we raised the issue of the interference of Iran in the life of Iraq through Shia brigades.

I know that this scholar denounced the Shias in Iran but rather more briefly in comparison with the diatribe of the morning. It was made abundantly clear that Ahmed Zaki Al Qasy had limited time for us. Thanks to the tirade at the Shia mosque we had arrived later than the prearranged hour, and this Sunni scholar had a further meeting to attend.

At about 4.00 pm we made polite farewells, returned past the ornamental pools and retrieved our cameras from the guards. From the car park we photographed the mosque and a small party of children entering the mosque area. Tom later recalled that a suspicious character was watching us. I did not see him. Cameras in hand, we climbed back into our vehicle and drove out, pausing to say a final word of thanks to the Sunni scholar who was seated in his car in the car park.

In our car the interpreter was in the front beside the driver. Immediately behind there were two rows of seats facing each other. Tom, Harmeet and Jim occupied these seats and I sat facing forwards in a third bench seat at the rear.

We drove down the road that led away from the mosque. A hundred yards on we swung left into an open area leading to the highway. Perhaps there was a fence to the right of the road but it was certainly exposed – a place in which kidnap was a real possibility although it was the last thing to enter our heads.

We were picking up speed when suddenly two cars cut in on us, a white Mercedes and another big car. They pulled up across our road. Our driver jammed on his brakes. Out of the cars leapt armed men. One had an automatic and the others were brandishing hand guns. All were in Western dress and clean shaven. One man wrenched open the driver's door and dragged him out, taking his place at the wheel. A second man opened the opposite door and pulled out the interpreter, demanding to know what he was doing with us, before jumping into the car with another man. One of the intruders pushed Jim to the floor between the two seats, saying 'get down' and sat almost on top of him. The other threw himself into the seat facing Tom and Harmeet but with his gun turned on me. This one looked rather nervous. The man dominating the others appeared much more of a tough, hardened kidnapper.

With the rogue driver in control we accelerated away. The whole thing had lasted perhaps 20 seconds. My last memory of driver and interpreter is of two figures standing forlornly at the roadside gazing after us, and getting smaller and smaller in the distance.

I was in a state of total disbelief. 'Can this be happening?' 'Is this what kidnap is like?' 'What is going to happen next?' Oddly enough, I felt curious rather than frightened; a strange disembodied state which was perhaps the result of shock. One of us produced the CPT 'magic sheet' which explains in English and Arabic our mission in Baghdad and pushed it into the hand of the man in command. He glanced at it but paid little attention.

The car sped along a highway without checkpoints and we turned off the main road into a residential area. I was too disorientated to follow the route but our captors were obviously determined to confuse us. Out of my rear window I spotted the same group of lads playing football in the road as we drove quickly past them for the second time. The car swung through a large steel gate and into the driveway of the building that we came to know as House No. 1.

We lurched to a halt and our captors wanted us to get out fast. The four of us were bundled through the doors at gunpoint. That was the last we saw of these kidnappers but we were obviously expected! Two men, probably those we came to call Medicine Man and Junior, ushered us through the front door and into a room measuring perhaps 15 by 25 feet with benches around the walls. We were handcuffed

[7]

individually, wrist to wrist in front of our bodies. Passports were taken from us as well as our cameras and my reading glasses. We gave out another copy of the magic sheet. They took Jim's gold watch but ignored the digital watches worn by Harmeet and myself. Perhaps we were actually blind-folded. I do not recall. My recollection of what happened in these first few days is poor.

At some stage in the first evening we were led into a second room on the ground floor measuring about 15 by 15 feet which had two beds and a row of plastic garden chairs. We sat down, handcuffed individually and facing the wall. At some stage we were provided with woolly hats which could be lowered over the eyes as a blindfold. We indicated that our captors should look more closely at the magic sheet. We may have produced yet another copy. I think that it was only now that they realised the sort of group we were and that the CPT did not pay ransom. Was there a muttered swear word in Arabic? I'm not sure. I understood from Tom that the men had speculated we might be Coalition spies who had been sent to discover their hideout. Our shoes and boots were removed – they were going to be examined for metal reflec-tor plates that could be used to signal to a helicopter! We saw them under the stairs for a few days and then they dis-appeared for ever, perhaps with Jim's watch via the souk? Harmeet was very concerned about the loss of his expensive pair of boots to the captors. I offered to buy him a new pair on release, a promise I have now happily been able to keep.

Later in the evening the man whom we came to call Medicine Man addressed us in reasonable English. We were apparently 'very fortunate' to have been kidnapped by Medicine Man's Mujahideen and not by the Zarkawi Mujahideen. He told us that the followers of Abu Musab al-Zarkawi would have immediately executed the American and the Briton – Tom and me. Later in the week we learned that followers of Zarkawi had offered to buy us but their offer had been refused. Only later did we discover that Medicine Man and his people belonged to a previously unknown group of Mujahideen guerrilla fighters who called themselves the Sword of Righteousness Brigade.

We were given water to drink, released to go to the *hammam* (toilet), taken back to the first room and allowed to lie down, the handcuffs still on our wrists. So that night we slept on a carpeted floor covered by a single thin blanket. Sleep was sporadic and we lay listening to all the sounds. At first there were the voices of our captors in the kitchen and then there was traffic noise, a train, dogs barking, a helicopter overhead. Dawn broke and we heard the muezzin, the call to prayer.

At a later stage in our confinement I wrote in my captivity notebook: 'Once I had a nightmare that I was kidnapped and confined, handcuffed to three others, in a small room, for weeks. I woke and it was reality.' I opened my eyes to see the dreadful truth of the room around me. I felt the handcuff on my wrist and the chain on my ankle. Why did I ever come to Iraq?

2

'HAVE BANNER, WILL TRAVEL'

If Jesus had said: 'Follow me and you will have comfort, wealth and possessions beyond the dreams of avarice', then we would have no need for commentaries by learned professors. We would say 'I understand full well what that means – I'll follow, and where do I collect the money?' But because Jesus actually says, 'Take up your cross and follow me', we suddenly find that we need commentaries and professors of biblical studies to tell us that Jesus didn't really mean, or even say, 'take up your cross' and, if he did, he didn't mean me!

Søren Kierkegaard

As a child of the 1930s I was brought up on a diet of the superiority of the British Empire with tales of its military and naval victories – we celebrated Empire Day properly at school. The Second World War broke out when I was eight and as a family, Mother, Grandma, my brother and I spent long periods in the west of England at Teignmouth while my father worked in London as a managing electrician. So at that time I came more under the influence of my mother's quiet propriety than my father's nonconformity and quixotic generosity. At Teignmouth we lived in a small bungalow on rough ground half way up a cliff with a view of the sea. On occasions we played war games with my two cousins!

When at home, near Wembley in north-west London, I was sent to Sunday School at Kingsbury Baptist Church, where a regular part of the teaching was about 'heroes of the faith'. These heroes – and some heroines – were mainly British missionaries like Dr David Livingstone, Mary Slessor of Calabar in Nigeria and William Carey, who undertook all manner of hazardous journeys to distant places in obedience to the call to preach the gospel. There were a series of books – the Eagle Books – which we could borrow to find out more about the lives of these courageous saints, with titles like *If Only I Had a Ship* (about John Williams of the South Seas).

As a teenager, just after the close of the Second World War in 1945, I remember going to rallies in London to hear Pastor Niemöller, who endured long years of captivity under the Nazi regime, and the outstanding Japanese Christian Toyohiko Kagawa who founded the Anti-War League. I will never forget his challenge at the end of his talk: 'Are you willing to become a tramp for Christ?'

These models of Christian discipleship were reinforced later on when I read *The Cost of Discipleship* by the German pastor Dietrich Bonhoeffer, who was hanged by the Gestapo on the special orders of Himmler in April 1945. In this book Bonhoeffer wrote about Cheap Grace – accepting the solace of Christianity without being prepared for costly obedience. He lived out his teaching by returning from a safe teaching post in the USA to his people in Germany just at the outbreak of war in 1939. Later, I recall studying this book with a small group in the USA at Mount Sinai Church, Long Island in the early 1960s. After three sessions we decided that since we were not prepared to live Christianity to this standard, it was hypocrisy to continue our studies. Such challenges to radical discipleship, then, are part of my consciousness but are

Dietrich Bonhoeffer (1906–1945)

usually well sublimated by my desire to live a normal life. My wife and I have a friend who gently mocks my tendency towards 'hair-shirt' Christian living.

At university in Exeter I studied for a degree in physics and during the first year left the generally prescriptive Christian Union to become a keen member of the more open and questioning Student Christian Movement. I had been persuaded that one function of university life was to enable one to explore the bases of all assumptions of belief.

For the first year I shared a room with two people who remain my friends to this day. Aubrey Scrase was a Methodist who had been in the Army in Burma, while Alan Ingram became a Quaker while at college. I immersed myself in student life at Exeter, taking an active part in cross country running and in 'Rag Week' (one year I made a mat of rubber 'nails' and sat on it dressed as a fakir in a loincloth). I think that I discovered myself at Exeter, perhaps through the hours of discussion – lively debate would be a better description. I would like to think that I left college with the enthusiasm of the Methodist and the ethics of the Quaker, so that when my call up papers arrived for National Service in 1952 I registered as a conscientious objector. My family accepted this decision, although my elder brother had done his National Service in the RAF. I had no problems arguing my case at the tribunal in London at Fulham Town Hall. I remember that you were expected to have read a book against pacifism (Isaac

Out running in my student days

Jolly's *Pacifism at the Bar of Holy Scripture and History* was the standard volume). I surprised the tribunal by having read some writings of former Archbishop of Canterbury William Temple that dismissed the pacifist position. Fortunately, objections to military service on Christian grounds seemed to be readily acceptable and I emerged from the tribunal with a direction to do alternative medical work for two years.

I took posts as a hospital porter (cleaning Matron's shoes at night) and a ward orderly (cleaning the urine bottles). Then I bent the rules by applying for and accepting a post as trainee physicist in the Radiotherapy Department at Scunthorpe War Memorial Hospital. Posts in medical physics were rare. Both the people who interviewed me for this post were sympathetic to my position as a conscientious objector. and in fact one was a leading member of the Christian pacifist organisation, the Fellowship of Reconciliation. At Scunthorpe I lodged with a family where the father was a carpenter for the council so that I gained, at second hand, some insight into the lives of the steelworkers in the town's council estates. After completing my training at Scunthorpe I came back to London and met for the first time the physicist and anti-nuclear weapons campaigner Joseph Rotblat (in the 1950s the effect of fall-out from nuclear bomb testing was a 'hot' topic).

Professor Rotblat was based at St Bartholomew's Hospital Medical School. In 1955 he interviewed me for a junior hospital physics post with duties at Barts and at the North Middlesex Hospital. At Barts I spent a lot of time in the Isotope Department where I worked on the detailed analysis of urine samples from patients with thyroid disorders. This was a method that Joe Rotblat had devised and written up. I was eventually able to demonstrate that a much simpler test was just as useful as a diagnostic tool although it took some time to persuade the professor of the validity of that fact.

In 1957 I felt that the time had come to make a move and

very nearly took a post in a missionary hospital in India. However I was easily persuaded to give up this project and to advance my career through research. Rotblat was disappointed that I did not stay at Barts to take his MSc course but I went off to the Royal Marsden in 1957 to work for my PhD. A research grant was provided by the British Electrical Industry in the expectation that I would seek a career in health physics at a nuclear power station. After three years of experimentation, I submitted my PhD in 1960 on the effects of radiation on bone growth. Theses are supposed to be of a length that can be read on the train from Cambridge to London. My examiner must have slept on the journey, judging by the lack of relevant questions put to me. I was hoping for a searching examination of my research, and found it unsatisfactory to be asked so little about my scientific labours. But he did award me a pass.

Back in London I had joined in the life of the Kingsbury Baptist Church, including the lively youth group. Pat Cartwright was also a member – attractive, sociable and much sought after by young men. She was a primary school teacher and was working at a school in Harrow.

Pat had already been converted to pacifism by our outspoken Baptist minister in Kingsbury, the Revd Walter Macdonald. He was a great human being. He had considered that to put on a chaplain's military uniform and take an oath to the monarch would compromise his primary loyalty to God. During the Second World War he exercised his pastoral ministry to the troops through the YMCA. In 1961 he proposed that the Baptist Union adopt a resolution 'That as Christians, we are forbidden to wage war'. Ironically, it was opposed by an army chaplain and defeated by a substantial majority.

In February 1957 I plucked up the courage to invite Pat Cartwright out to a film on St Valentine's Day. It was *War and*

Peace. I told her that I was inviting her out 'seriously' and she accepted. She told me afterwards that it had taken her a long time to get to know me because I was so reserved and lacking in social graces. Pat's mother made no bones about the fact that she thought I was eccentric and not sociable enough for her attractive daughter. My mother, on the other hand, thought Pat was too frivolous for her clever son! After a gentle courtship with poetry and presents I stopped the motorbike when taking her to school one morning in 1959 and proposed. To my delight she accepted me.

Pat and I were married by Walter Macdonald at Kingsbury Baptist Church in September 1960 and went straight off to start married life in the United States. In those days it was almost expected that a grant for post-doctoral studies in the United States would be forthcoming after a research degree. I had been offered a grant for a year's research at the Brookhaven National Laboratory on Long Island, where I worked in the biology laboratory. It was a very enjoyable year, but I produced little useful science.

On one occasion a group of anti-nuclear campaigners took their stand outside the laboratory gates. On my way into the site I stopped to talk to them and explained that, as far as I knew, no war-related research was undertaken in the laboratory. The Brookhaven security guards came to take my details. This was the post-Joseph McCarthy era of anti-communist witch hunting but there were no ill consequences.

Pat and I lived, first of all, on the laboratory site, and then moved to a small but delightful one-storey house on the North Shore of Long Island. We attended an old white weather-boarded congregational church. I remember talking to church groups in nearby towns about Christian pacifism and being regarded with absolute incomprehension – it was a completely new topic to them. At that time pacifism was seen as un-American, particularly by church members who saw it

*With the Revd Walter Macdonald at our wedding in
September 1960*

as their duty to serve in the National Guard (the US equivalent of the Territorial Army). My wife recalls that at one of
these meetings a man argued that the United States should
have 'nuked' Russia while they had the chance – i.e. before
retaliation was possible.

In 1961 we left the USA and returned to London where I
was accepted for a teaching post in the Physics Department

at the Royal Free Medical School. Pat and I bought a house in north-west London at Harrow and after our two daughters, Sally and Joanna, were born we moved to neighbouring Pinner.

In 1973 I took the post of Reader in Physics at St Bartholomew's Hospital School of Medicine under my former mentor, Joe Rotblat. Joe was a first class lecturer in addition to his many other accomplishments and the students always enjoyed his lectures. He went to great lengths to set up demonstrations for them and some of his experiments with radioactive sources would never be allowed today!

Joe was Polish and had participated in the atomic bomb project in the USA until it became known that the Germans would never produce a nuclear weapon and that bombs were being developed in anticipation of a threat from Russia. Joe promptly resigned. After the war he had joined a group of scientists from both East and West who were arguing for an end to nuclear weapons, and helped to found the annual series of conferences on arms control in Pugwash, Nova Scotia. Ultimately he became President of the Pugwash Conferences and was awarded the Nobel Peace Prize in 1994.

Joe's opposition to nuclear weapons and his belief that war could be abolished were based on pragmatic grounds. He gave the impression that he regarded my involvement with Christian pacifists as a poor second to the humanitarian mission. He wished me to join the British Pugwash movement but I knew that my knowledge of nuclear physics was so poor that I could make no useful contribution to its work.

At Barts the academic Department of Physics was kept separate from the Hospital Department of Physics and it was this policy that was partly responsible for the eventual closure of the academic side. The other cause of closure was the fact that I was appointed Head of Department when Joe retired. He was a very hard act to follow and I was not in Joe's league as either a scientist or an administrator, although he always tolerated me kindly. When I took over I tried to run the department democratically, a move which was resented by many of the staff who preferred Joe's autocratic rule. The secretary left after a year, telling me that life with me was too dull!

Thus I remained in medically-related research and teaching throughout my career. For my continuing studies of the mechanisms of bone growth, which included the making of one of the first computer-animated films, I was awarded a Doctorate of Science in 1974. I retired from university teaching in 1992 as a Professor of Biophysics.

Meanwhile, having made the decision to register as a conscientious objector in 1952, I went on to become active in the inter-church peace movement, the Fellowship of Reconciliation (FoR). For a short time I led its youth group in London. I was also a member of the committee of the Baptist Peace Fellowship (BPF) where, I am ashamed to say, I was rather critical of some of the older members for their lack of activism.

When Pat and I became engaged she joined me on an Aldermaston 'Ban the Bomb' march in 1959. I had a motor cycle in the 1950s and I recall riding with Pat on the pillion (another black mark from her mother) along the road from Reading to Aldermaston with a CND symbol on the balloon tied to the luggage rack. I made my first banner that year – 'Baptists on the March' – using enlarged letters cut from *The Times* as templates with the lettering in white emulsion on blue cloth. Pat and I always marched with the Christian groups and had lively conversations *en route*. As usual the press gave no publicity to the Christian presence on the marches but gave extended coverage to the small but rowdy hippy contingent. The songs of those days are wonderfully evocative of the camaraderie of those marches:

Men and women join together,
do not heed the men of war,
make your minds up now or never
ban the bomb for evermore!

The basis of the FoR is a call to radical discipleship. I found
myself once again faced with the dilemma of wanting to follow the demands of the gospel but at the same time wishing
to live a normal life with Pat, Sally and Joanna. I made card-

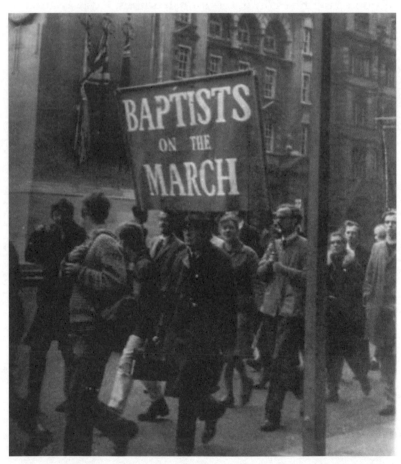

Baptists on the March from Aldermaston in 1962

With Sally, Pat and Joanna, 1981

board slide rules to help them in learning tables, a computer story with missing words and a board game of railway journeys around Britain. I also enjoyed making up stories for them. One concerned the adventures of 'Albert the Bath'. This started me off on my hobby of collecting over 200 photographs of recycled baths in the countryside.

During the 1960s I found myself unwilling to live up to a challenging standard of discipleship and thus fell away from both the FoR and the BPF to pursue my career and family life as a comfortable member of a Baptist Church. I taught in Sunday School and helped at a club for children. It took me until the 1980s to accept that none can fully live up to the high calling of being followers of Jesus – of being called Christians.

[21]

Having come to that realisation and acceptance I felt able to rejoin the FoR and BPF and during the 1980s I became active in Christian CND – the Campaign for Nuclear Disarmament – during the crisis years when Reagan and Thatcher were heating up the Cold War. Pat and I have powerful memories of the demonstration outside the Atomic Weapons Establishment in the South of England at Burghfield. After a time of prayer a Dominican friar produced a large pair of wire cutters from under his black cape and proceeded to snip his way into the base where he knelt in prayer. The security guards appeared promptly but since the base was not marked on Ordnance Survey maps it was not possible to prosecute someone for trespassing on property that does not exist! I also joined a number of demonstrations at various military bases and was almost rent-a-demonstrator – 'Have banner, will travel'. On one march in London, probably on Hiroshima Day, Pat and I lay down in the road for a 10-minute 'die in' on Oxford Street.

When I retired from university teaching in 1992 I decided to give up science for voluntary work with the Christian peace movements. I rejoined the committee of the Baptist Peace Fellowship and worked in the FoR office. Through membership of the Network of Christian Peace Organisations I became well known among peace activists of all denominations and am a Trustee of the Roman Catholic Pax Christi Peace Education Fund.

Much of the literature on Christian peacemaking seemed too cerebral, so I wrote a number of simple pamphlets: *A Rough Guide to Christian Peacemaking, What about Mrs Goliath?* and *Can you be a Christian and a Patriot?*. My favourite is a publication by the 'University of Hell' – a dissertation for the Diploma in Obfuscation on 'Objections to Christian Peacemaking'. In this I followed the pattern of C. S. Lewis's *Screwtape Letters* and argued as devil's advocate. The dissertation claims that although a basic reading of the Gospels teaches non-violence, young Christians should accept the excuses used by the church since the time of the Emperor Constantine (312 AD) and reject pacifism. My devil argues that pacifism isn't biblical, historical or practical and always tries to confuse pacifism with passive-ism, and to identify positive non-violent action with apathy and appeasement.

On two trips abroad I endeavored to mix science with peacemaking and visited Baptists in Hungary (1976) and the Ukraine (1982) while giving lectures on bone growth to research groups in those countries. In 1988 Pat and I attended a Baptist peace gathering in Sweden and four years later I went to a follow-up meeting in Nicaragua. From there I flew north to El Salvador and stayed with two sisters of the Roman Catholic Congregation of St Joseph of Peace. They took me to see the church where Archbishop Oscar Romero had been murdered for his outspoken criticism of the El Salvador regime and his support of the common people. A humbling experience.

Before it was brought to an untimely end by the withdrawal of funds, I was a member of the interdenominational Churches Peace Forum and with them I went on visits to the Faslane Trident base in Scotland, to Bradford University School of Peace Studies and to NATO headquarters at Brussels. On this last visit we had a session with NATO military officers and I remember a chilling response to one question. I asked how they changed fighters into peacekeepers. The Norwegian and British officers replied that they had learned from experience and quoted the example of the United Nations peacekeeping force in Cyprus. The United States officer answered that American men do not join their military services to do *peace* duties but for active combat (not to pat heads but to kick butts!).

For a number of years I joined the workers in the Peace

Zone at the Greenbelt Christian Arts Festival. This festival is held over the August public holiday each year and attracts up to 20,000 young people – mainly for the loud modern Christian music. I found that in order to get the attention of young people you generally had to be innovative and zany. In addition to writing basic pamphlets I had tried to float a polystyrene dove on helium balloons (I forgot about the wind!) and made giant hands ('Peace is in your hands') and a peace dragon. In 2005 the festival took place on Cheltenham race course and I walked around dressed as a Peace Tree, asking festival-goers to tie leaves with messages of peace onto my branches.

In 2003 I carried our Baptist Peacemakers banner as one of over a million people who marched and demonstrated in London against involving Britain in a war against Iraq. I feel that the message on that occasion was too negative and that not enough thought had been given to putting forward positive ideas for bringing down Saddam Hussein without the use of violence. Since the West had supported him in the past it should have been possible to find ways to depose him without using the punitive sanctions which had dire effects on the Iraqi population and little or no effect – even the reverse – on the dictator himself, and had in fact strengthened his position, since he was able to excuse his tyranny as a necessary response to Iraq's enemies.

A special interest of mine had become the history of non-violence and I had become a keen evangelist arguing that Christians should show a much greater interest in and enthusiasm for non-violent victories. Through my various peace activities I encountered the Mennonites, one of the Historic Peace Churches. In 1984 the American Mennonite Ron Sider had challenged his denomination to be prepared to give their lives in developing new non- violent attempts to reduce international conflict:

We must take up our cross and follow Jesus to
Golgotha ... Those who have believed in peace
through the sword have not hesitated to die ...
Unless we are ready to die developing new non-
violent attempts to reduce international conflict,
we should confess that we never really meant the
cross was an alternative to the sword.

Christian Peacemaker Teams arose as a result of that call
and was initiated by Mennonites, Brethren and Quakers in
the USA and Canada out of their concern to devote the same
discipline and self-sacrifice to non-violent peacemaking that
armies devote to war. They seek non-violent alternatives to
war. Among their other activities, CPT place violence-
reduction teams in crisis situations and militarised areas
around the world at the invitation of local peace and human
rights workers.

In March 2005 the Mennonite Centre in London
arranged a day's workshop about Christian Peacemaker
Teams. I was interested and decided to attend. The day was led
by William Payne, a Canadian, who had seen service with the
CPT in Israel, Colombia, Mexico and with First Nation
Americans in Ontario. Although I was well aware that none
of us can fully live up to the high calling of following Jesus,
William Payne re-awoke all my concerns about being a
'cheap' peacemaker. Was I enjoying the consolations of
Christianity without living up to its commitment? Here I
was, a comfortable retired academic conscientious objector
who talked, wrote and demonstrated about peace. In no way
was I taking risks for my beliefs in the way that young
servicemen and women in Iraq were taking risks for theirs. I
sought in vain for reasons why I should *not* become involved
with CPT. I found none. I decided to explore the possibility
of gaining experience of CPT work, not as a full member, but

by joining a short-term delegation. That decision was to lead me to Iraq and into kidnap.

I went to Iraq with three modest aims:

1: to meet Iraqi people and assure them many in the West regretted the war.

2: to discover how Christian Peacemaker Teams worked in practice and whether they were suitable guardians for young people from FoR we might wish to sponsor on peacemaking projects.

3: to prove that at 74 I was not past taking adventures in my Christian peacemaking.

3

JORDAN AND BAGHDAD

My role was to bear witness to the suffering of the Iraqi people living under a harsh military occupation ... and, as a Westerner, to offer a sense of solidarity to the Iraqi people.

Harmeet Singh Sooden

CPT logo

I did not decide to join CPT as a full member – nor have I to this day. Over the summer of 2005 I gradually worked out, a step at a time, the best way forward. I looked up possibilities on the CPT website and decided that my destination would be either Israel/Palestine or Iraq. A number of friends had been to Israel/Palestine with Pax Christi and Christian Aid to report on the situation there, so I perversely chose Iraq. I discussed my intention with a Canadian Baptist, Lee McKenna Du Charme, who had served with CPT and she confirmed that even a brief experience of CPT at work would be valuable in fulfilling my own limited aims.

I submitted my curriculum vitae to the head office of the CPT at Chicago in July and gave the names of referees who would confirm my commitment to peace work. The delegation was due to go to Baghdad via Jordan from 19 November to 2 December 2005 (14 days). I sat back to await news from Chicago and a letter of acceptance arrived in August to be followed by a large package of documentation:

- 13 items of essential information on travel, health (including the risks associated with depleted uranium), cultural notes, a sexual harassment policy and a sheet of words and phrases in Arabic.
- 19 items on CPT work in Iraq, including details of the current situation, past delegation reports, an Occupation timeline, an overview of Iraqi history, a report on UN sanctions and an introduction to Islam.

I made arrangements for the delegate's fee to be paid to the CPT office in Chicago and, using the internet, I booked a return flight to Amman with British Airways. The purchase of tickets for the flight from Jordan to Baghdad was the responsibility of CPT. My total costs were about £1,000.

I gently broke the news of my desire to go with the CPT delegation to Pat and she was not happy – to put it mildly. In trying to reassure her I reminded her that I would only be away for 14 days! She appreciated that this was probably my last chance to undertake such a venture.

We consulted our minister, who was against the trip because of the stress it would put on Pat. He suggested a visit to my general practitioner for medical advice, in the hope that the doctor would advise against it. The GP saw no reason on health grounds why I should not travel and changed my blood pressure medication from a diuretic to beta blockers because the beta blockers would help to relieve stress. This change must have helped my mental condition during the long period of captivity.

In October, partly to ease my conscience at leaving Pat, we did go on a trip to Madeira for a week, and in spite of the treat of taking tea at Reid's Palace Hotel in Funchal, I felt a certain shadow of Iraq over that holiday.

I followed the CPT advice, sorted out the necessary range of clothes for variable weather and temperatures and borrowed a rucksack from my son-in-law so that I could travel light and, if necessary, carry all my effects on to a flight.

On 19 November two friends kindly drove Pat and me to Heathrow. We said a brief farewell outside the terminal where cars are allowed to pause to unload. I wanted it to be a low-key farewell so that Pat was not too distressed. After all, I was only going to be away for 13 nights. She tells me that she feared that I might be shot or killed in a bombing incident but the possibility of kidnap did not occur to her. We were both aware that nine previous CPT delegations had visited Iraq without any problems and returned safely.

British Airways then took me on the four-and-a-half hour flight to the Queen Alia airport in Amman. There I followed the precise instructions supplied by CPT and went to the entry desk to pay the visa fee for Jordan before taking the airport bus (a cheaper option than a taxi) to the centre of Amman.

The Al Monzer Hotel is in the same square as the bus terminal but I had to cross a very busy road which seems to be the base for many Amman taxi services. The Al Monzer must be the scruffiest hotel I have ever stayed in. As I climbed the

View from the Al Monzer Hotel, Amman

stairs, I was aware that each corner of the staircase was filled with the rubbish of the years. I came into a large space with the hotel reception desk at one end and a spread of tables and easy chairs everywhere else. There was a television set against the far wall. I introduced myself to the man behind the desk and negotiated to avoid a shared room – useful for my ease of mind, both because I snore and because I like to get up and read in the middle of the night. (It was an ironic request in the light of my sleeping arrangements for the next three-and-a-half months!)

My room looked out to the rear of the hotel onto a slope well laden with old cans and plastic bags, among which some hens came to peck for food. At the top of the slope were apartment blocks. I have slept in cleaner rooms but there were basic en suite facilities and at the back of the hotel it must have been considerably quieter than in the rooms overlooking the road at the front. In the morning I encountered a large pool of water in the corridor outside – a leaky roof? In favour of the Al Monzer, I understand that the management and staff have always been helpful to CPT members and delegates in terms of providing them with information and making email facilities available.

Having taken the precaution of including two packets of cereal and some chocolate milk in my rucksack I started breakfast before descending to the main room. The other members of the delegation were already eating and drinking and so I came to meet my companions for the next four months.

Originally there were to be five in the group but one lady from Florida had withdrawn some weeks before the departure date. So at 10.00 am on the morning of Sunday 20 November four people gathered for our first meeting. Our leader, James Loney, was in his early forties. Rather taller than I, he preferred the checked shirts of a backwoodsman, and was, in fact, the coordinator of CPT in Canada. This was not his first trip to Iraq. He had previously served with the team there and also in Hebron. Jim was a trained mediator and a support worker for the CPT project in Kenora, Ontario where they work with First Nation people. Before joining CPT he had belonged to the Catholic Worker movement in Canada.

Harmeet Singh Sooden from New Zealand was another Canadian by nationality – a young engineer in his early thirties of Kashmiri background. He was about my height but much slimmer and fitter. Harmeet had worked as an engineer in Auckland but had changed direction to study English Literature at university and intended to become a teacher. He had documented the effects of the military occupation in Kashmir and military equipment production in New

Zealand. He had also worked as a fundraiser for a school in Zambia and volunteered with the International Solidarity Movement in Palestine.

Then in addition to myself there was someone whom I will call the fourth man. We were given our itinerary for the delegation: two days in Jordan, the flight to Baghdad, nine days in Iraq including trips south to Najaf and Kerbala, before the return to Amman for flights home.

Jim, Harmeet and I were fairly cautious in our initial approaches to each other, not wishing to impress our own personalities on the working of the group. This was not the case with the fourth man, who was keen to let us know all about his previous visit to Iraq with a different organisation before the 2003 war.

Our first appointment that morning was to meet Peter Dula, a young American who coordinates the Iraq programme for the Mennonite Central Committee. We joined him in the Moorish-style coffee room of the rather up-market Toledo Hotel next door to the Al Monzer.

Here the fourth man revealed himself as someone who had not come to listen but to expound his views on the current situation in Iraq. He embarrassed us by his denunciations of the Coalition policy in a voice that was so loud that everyone in the room turned to listen.

Our next expedition within Amman was to the carefully protected office of the Human Rights division of the International Committee of the Red Cross. We were to become accustomed to armed guards checking papers before admission to any office. Upstairs we were introduced to the deputy head of the delegation and to the officer responsible for tracing missing persons. The Human Rights division arranges visits by relatives to people in detention and also the delivery of humanitarian parcels. They have to work from their office in Jordan since the ICRC left Baghdad when their headquarters were bombed. The fourth man fell asleep during the conversations we had with the ICRC staff.

We walked back to the hotel just as groups of young people were coming out of college. On one side of the road was a very extensive building site and on the other various commercial premises. We also passed an Orthodox church and I went to look in at the door and saw a large crowd of worshippers. The others did not join me so I caught up and walked on with them. There are at least two traditions of Orthodoxy in Jordan and I think this church was of the Greek order. Back in our square we joined a crowded bar that sold falafel – small spicy chickpea balls. Harmeet queued up to place our order and we ate them standing under cover from the rain.

That night we climbed up a long flight of steps to a restaurant in a hilly area behind the Al Monzer Hotel and had a fine view over the city. The room was largely empty and when we settled at a table the fourth man sat apart from us and did not enter into the conversation at all. It was evident to Jim that he had a difficult decision to make. Back at the hotel Jim made a call to consult with the CPT head office in Chicago and it was agreed that the fourth man was not to proceed to Baghdad. He protested but the decision was final as Jim had responsibility for our conduct and safety in Iraq.

The following day our scheduled trip was to the United Nations Human Rights office, which involved a taxi journey out of the city towards the airport. Again, the building was heavily fortified and we had to pass through security checks before we were able to meet with John Pace, Human Rights Chief for the UN Assistance Mission in Iraq (UNAMI). John is a Maltese Australian and had previously served as Secretary to the United Nations Commission on Human Rights. It was extremely interesting to meet him and the members of his team. Unfortunately the detailed notes I made of the meeting were lost at the kidnap but I well remember that John Pace and his team were grateful for the information the CPT team were able to provide because CPT were on the ground and outside the secure Green Zone in Baghdad. CPT had developed a wide range of contacts in Baghdad and were able to report evidence from victims of physical abuse in detention.

It was pouring with rain when we left the UN office and we got soaked in the five minutes before we were able to hail a taxi. The final visit of that Monday was to Fr Denis Como of the Jesuits, who have a house in Amman. They work with Iraqi refugees of the Chaldean Catholic Church who have made their way into Jordan. Jordan does not welcome these refugees, and they find it very difficult to obtain residence and work permits.

The area around the Al Monzer had some fine mosques but we did not have a chance to visit them. Fortunately Pat and I had visited Amman previously on a church trip to Jordan and Israel in 1994, so I had seen many of the major tourist sights of the city. The road outside the hotel was pretty scruffy, with disjointed pavements outside taxi offices, a pharmacist, a chicken kebab kitchen and various other small shops. As we dodged round the obstacles we encountered a mixture of smells including barbecued chicken and tyres! A few hundred yards towards the centre of town we selected a basic cafe for an evening snack – I have forgotten what we ate but it was something that seemed simple and safe.

Early on the Tuesday morning we took a taxi to Amman's small Marka airport. We arrived before it was fully open and had to wait for the luggage scanners to be switched on. There were few facilities; just a tiny shop providing some basic necessities and a few cuddly camels and a man behind a bar providing a limited range of food and drink.

We flew into Baghdad in a small plane run by Air Serv

The Air Serv plane which took us from Amman to Baghdad

International, a non-profit humanitarian organisation that use their own aircraft to provide safe, reliable and cost-effective air transport to other humanitarian agencies. Air Serv are prepared to fly where other air carriers cannot or will not go and our small plane had about 25 seats.

As we took off, there were fine views over Amman; the city is set on hills clad in white and sand-coloured houses. Flying east, there was little to see over the Iraqi desert and then we began the spiral descent into Baghdad airport. This corkscrew landing, largely over the airport grounds, is performed to reduce the risk of rocket attack.

As we descended there was another small plane landing and out of this came a group of macho-looking security men. Once down safely, our passage through the airport was facilitated within an hour or so by Greg Rollins, a Canadian from British Columbia, who had come out from the CPT apartment to bring our clearance documents. Without Greg it would have taken us several hours to get clear of the airport and all the checks.

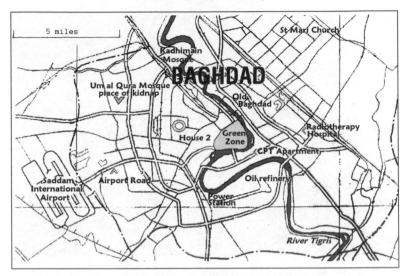

Map of Baghdad

We drove away in two special airport cars that are recognised at the checkpoint on the airport perimeter and we did not have to stop. Thus we approached Baghdad on the infamous airport road where there have been too many shootings and bombings.

The airport road runs through wide open dusty spaces with the occasional concrete checkpoint; every so often a machine gun post appeared over a perimeter wall and there was no shortage of burnt-out cars. Although there were groves of palm trees we saw plenty of the dull brown scenery of desolation that is the familiar backdrop to TV reports of military action. As we approached the city the roads were lined with rather run-down buildings. Most of them appeared to be linked to some trading function and the general impression was less than salubrious.

Colour, however, was added in the form of posters for the forthcoming election and these were pasted onto every available hoarding and stretch of wall. There was evidently a plethora of political parties.

The streets grew narrower, and turning towards the river we had our first sight of the CPT apartment block. This is an unremarkable building of four storeys with well-barred windows at street level. The members of the permanent Christian Peacemaker Team live on the ground floor and, as delegation members, we were to be accommodated in a large apartment on the top floor up three flights of stairs. With an unreliable power supply it was not sensible to use the lift.

I again had a room to myself – considerable luxury compared with our subsequent accommodation – while Jim and Harmeet shared the accommodation next door. I unpacked and went down to the spacious living/dining room in the CPT apartment for introductions. At that time the full team in Baghdad consisted of Greg Rollins, who had come to meet us and three Americans: Anita David, a Presbyterian from Chicago who was of Assyrian descent (her great-grandfather had been a Presbyterian minister in Iran); Maxine Nash, a Quaker from Iowa and Tom Fox from Virginia, also a Quaker. We were given safety advice: don't go wandering by ourselves, don't walk in large groups and avoid, as far as possible, drawing attention to the fact that we were Westerners. Once the introductions and early warnings were over, team and visiting delegation sat down together round a large table and shared our first meal.

Tom Fox was the most retiring of the CPT members, a quiet presence in the background although he evidently held strong views. The day before our kidnap he wrote on the CPT computer:

We are here to root out all aspects of dehumanisation that exist within us. We are here to stand with those being dehumanised by oppressors and stand firm against the dehumanisation. We are here to stop people, including ourselves from dehumanising any of God's children, no matter how much they dehumanise their own souls.

The living/dining room was sizeable and included some large sofas and a coffee table. The corridor outside led to the library/computer room, team members' bedrooms, the kitchen and the bathroom. I wasted no time in settling down at the computer to send an email to our minister in Harrow, Bob Gardiner to send love to Pat and say that I had arrived in a safeish area of Baghdad ready for the next ten days.

Once my email was safely away, I accompanied Maxine into the nearby shopping street where we walked past a range of shops to one that repaired mobile phones. Maxine wore the hajib and told me to walk slowly as it was not the Iraqi habit to hurry. Outside every other shop there seemed to be small red generators for emergency electrical supply, sitting on the edge of the pavement with cables crossing the path. The side road leading to the CPT apartment was festooned with cables. If the supply failed in your house a neighbour might be able to supply you from his power.

The shops appeared to be well stocked, with goods piled high in general disorder, and we paused at one to buy batteries. Each shop was small; I saw no large ones and they reminded me of small convenience corner stores in Britain. By contrast, the pharmacies and opticians were large, bright and well laid out with shop fittings in Western style.

As evening drew on we discovered the need to carry a torch with us as the power was liable to fail at any time. I slept badly that first night because of the noisy generator outside the offices across the street and tried to read the Agatha Christie novel *They Came to Baghdad*. I gave up when I decided that I wasn't bothered which of the cardboard characters was killed or who had done it.

Earlier in the evening we had made a trip to the roof of the apartment block. This offered a wonderful panorama across our section of Baghdad with views across the River Tigris to the Green Zone – now known as the International Zone – which housed the Coalition authorities and included the main palaces of Saddam Hussein.

On the roof of the CPT building was a reminder of the dangers of life in this city in the shape of new water tanks – the old ones had been destroyed by a stray mortar shell. It was aiming for the Green Zone but fell short onto the CPT building. There were also signs of shell damage nearby and in the derelict building next door I spotted a family with children living among the wreckage on the ground floor.

The following morning Jim, Harmeet and I made our own breakfasts in our kitchen upstairs. Prayers for all CPT members, staff and delegates were held in the large lounge on the top floor. We then made our way downstairs where a car was waiting for us.

We drove away southwards to one of Baghdad's power stations. On the route I recall seeing a number of burnt-out cars and there was heavy protection in place around police stations. Harmeet nearly caused an incident by his conspic-uous photographing of all that interested him – which was most things. We had just passed a police station when two men in plain clothes stepped out and stopped us. They said they were police and we had been seen taking pictures of the police station. The driver explained that we were foreigners and did not know any better. The men told the driver not to let it happen again.

The four chimneys of the power station came into sight, dominating the horizon. Just one of them was belching out smoke as we drove through the security barriers, presented our credentials, deposited our cameras and entered the main office building. Here we were met by Mr Safa'a Hussain, who

The Al Dura power station with its four chimneys

is the manager of the plant. He received us courteously and we explained briefly who we were and where we came from. Our questions on the present functioning of the plant and its failure to deliver a sufficient supply to keep the lights of Baghdad on for much more than six hours a day were listened to and answered carefully. The trouble was that the answers did not quite add up! We were left with various doubts. Among these was the exact function of the contractors from the US firm Bechtel, who apparently had a contract to refurbish two of the four oil-burning generators. We were given the impression that Bechtel's foreign workforce were not in any hurry to complete the task and that it would have been better to employ Iraqi engineers. We were also told that the four gas-fired generators could not be used due to insufficient gas pressure, which appeared to be blamed on the insurgents who bombed the gas pipe lines.

Mr Safa'a told us that a further two power stations were in the planning stage but gave no solid information on their likely start date let alone when they might be finished. The meeting ended with some pleasantries about the career of his son, presently at school, but without any indication that there had been fatherly advice about life in the electrical engineering industry! There were apparently no jobs for graduates in Iraqi firms.

Afterwards we were taken into the workshops of the maintenance crew who were trying to refurbish the second of the oil-burning generators. Here we met a cheerful group of engineers and technicians who were doing their best with inadequate equipment and were anxious to know what we were doing in Iraq. They were keen to explain to us that the members of this crew were all from different backgrounds. They got on perfectly well and they told us that divisions between sects were much overplayed by the West. We noticed a grassed area opposite the workshops where workers were playing football or relaxing.

Our final expedition took us into the bowels of the earth under a bomb safety bunker shaped like a pyramid. We were invited into the tearoom, where we met the foreman of the safety crew and some of his staff. The foreman complained that there was insufficient emphasis on safety and told us that two of the staff had fallen to their deaths while undertaking steeplejack work without safety harnesses. He said he was short of basic items like helmets and safety boots and there was no equipment to detect dangerous gases.

In spite of all the problems we were impressed by the friendliness of the foreman and his team, although they did seem to be somewhat past retiring age! It was good to be able to report that the workforce of the Baghdad power station were in good spirits in spite of the constraints on their work. They were not, however, able to suggest that we should be in any hurry to throw away the torches that are essential items of equipment in Baghdad after dark.

In the afternoon we made a visit on foot, walking in pairs, to visit the offices of the Iraqi Al-Amal Association. This Non-Governmental Organisation was created in 1992 and in May 2003 the Head Office was set up in Baghdad. Al-Amal provides a wide-ranging programme of activities and services, including work with women and the training of young people in conflict resolution techniques. The walls were decorated by colourful children's posters on the theme of peace and we witnessed a brief drama of conflict resolution played out by a rather shy group of teenagers. Our route back to the apartment building took us past St Raphael's Catholic Church, where CPT members often worshipped. Opposite the church was St Raphael's Hospital and both buildings were

Children's posters on the theme of peace at the Al-Amal Association offices

The Institute of Radiology

protected from car bombs by concrete blocks set up in the road outside.

On the way home there was a big bang from the other side of the river which made us jump. We were told it was the sound of unexploded devices being blown up.

The following morning we drove out to the Al-Dawrah oil refinery on a planned visit. A numbers of large oil tankers were going in and out as we waited for our letter of introduction to be approved but in the end permission to enter was denied. We also had hopes of an audience with members of the Iraqi Communist Party but they were too busy preparing for the forthcoming election. I acquired two of their election posters.

As a substitute I suggested a visit to the Institute of Radiology and Nuclear Medicine, since I had special knowledge of radiation medical physics. This idea was accepted by Jim and Harmeet, although I had little expectation that we would be admitted without the necessary permit from the Ministry of Health. We parked our car inside the security barrier of the hospital, made ourselves known and were led through the impressive square into the spotless modern building. To my surprise we were shown straight into the presence of the medical director of the Institute, Dr Abid Al Mehedi Kadhumi, who had been trained in London.

I was most interested to meet him and we discovered that this was the only radiotherapy treatment centre in Iraq. All treatments are carried out using two elderly cobalt-60 therapy machines (these are rarely used in Western hospitals, having been replaced by the much more convenient linear accelerators). Because the radioactive cobalt sources that produce the radiation had not been replaced for many years, the treatment times were tediously long so the machines were used on a four-shift-a-day pattern to maximise the throughput of patients. We learned that a state-of-the-art linear accelerator from Germany had been delivered and was awaiting installation in the Institute. We received no indication as to when that happy event would take place nor what might be the causes of the delay. We guessed that the specially-designed treatment room had yet to be built. We were introduced to the head of Radiation Physics who had been trained in Britain and who explained that they were struggling to do good physics with old equipment.

Since some of our visits had been cancelled we were taken on a drive round Baghdad to show us some of the principal sights. No great impression remains with me, since I always require a map to link sights with places. I have pleasant recollections of a few green spaces and some enclosed stands of palm trees. I know that we crossed the Tigris and viewed a range of fine old historic civic buildings from one of the bridges. Nearly all current government departments and the parliament, however, are sited safely in the Green Zone and therefore associated in the minds of Iraqis with the Coalition forces.

I also recall a stop in Mutanabi Street, named after a tenth century poet and specialising in literature. A range of books were spread out on tables and in boxes, reminding me of book sales on the riverside at the South Bank in London. Most of the books were in Arabic, with some text books and paperbacks in English. Passing on, we came to a road with old balconied houses and made a stop at a tea house where the walls were covered in old photographs of the city from the 1920s. We drank fruit juice standing up, as there were no seats.

Back in the CPT apartment, chores were carried out according to a rota. Meals were prepared in turn by one team member and one delegation member, the choice of food being up to the pair responsible for the meal. I arranged to get kidnapped on the Saturday to avoid my turn for this chore. I remember eating some excellent fish one evening and there was always lively conversation over the meal table. I caused a stir by my assertion that *The Lord of the Rings* trilogy was dangerous in that the enemies are invariably sub-human e.g. the Orcs. Thus they mirror all wars, which are an exercise in denying the humanity of the opposite side so that they can be treated as 'things'. Greg Rollins is a great fan of the trilogy and sprang to the defence of the books and films. Tom failed to support me and I was surprised in the light of his strong views on dehumanisation. Meals were followed by washing up – the second chore. I did this duty one evening.

On 25 November we prepared for a scheduled visit to Father Douglas Al-Bazi at the St Mari Chaldean Catholic Church in the Ur district. (St Mari was a disciple of St Addai, in turn a disciple of St Thomas the Apostle who brought Christianity to Iraq.)

This was a Friday morning, the Muslim Sabbath, so traffic was light as we sped through to North Baghdad. The church

Father Douglas with his flight of ducks

stands in the midst of an area of single storey housing. Outside
there are barriers and an armed guard. Inside we were welcomed by Father Douglas and taken up to his office on the
first floor; a comfortable room with a large desk and soft seating. Father Douglas sat beneath a flight of ceramic ducks and
we sat facing him.

We introduced ourselves and were, in turn, introduced to
Father Douglas' perspective on life as parish priest to 100
families. Twenty years ago there were 300 families in his
parish but many have opted for life with relatives in North
America or elsewhere. Father Douglas was a director of the
Christian Teaching Institute in Baghdad where 180 students
are following a six-year course at present. Only one or two

go on to the seminary to become priests. Father Douglas told us that at present there are 33 priests serving 24 Christian churches in Baghdad. He is naturally worried about the future, saying that the situation in Baghdad changes every six hours!

The Chaldean Catholic Church has a long history of persecution going back for generations. Trials under the Turks forced people to flee to the Mosul region and a further persecution brought people to Baghdad. The Christian population has fallen from the 1984 census figure of 1.4 million to an estimated 600,000 today.

The difficulties and hazards of daily life encouraged people to leave the country. Father Douglas obviously wanted them to remain and was concerned that those who left and then returned often brought sectarian divisions back with them. Attending his church at present he has Chaldean, Orthodox, Syrian, Armenian and other Christians all worshipping together. He told us that one of his parishioners, a police officer, had been shot and introduced us to a young schoolboy, Lawrence, who had been kidnapped on his way home from school! Lawrence was bundled into a car and driven away. The kidnappers telephoned Lawrence's father and told the boy to tell his father that he was being ill-treated (although he wasn't) and that the ransom was 200,000 dinars. A skilled worker might expect to take home 50,000 dinars per week; an unskilled person in the region of 25,000 dinars. In terms of purchasing power this buys very little. In the end a sum of 79,500 dinars was negotiated for Lawrence's release. Apparently the lad was properly fed and he was not ill treated by his captors. These days he always comes home from school in company with others. Another young lad had also been kidnapped – Father Douglas said this one was naughty and deserved it!

He told us of an attempt by car bombers which had been

thwarted by the guards (provided by the state). They discovered the bomb twenty minutes before a Mass which was
to be attended by the Chaldean Patriarch. By the time the
guards called the police and tried to evacuate the church and
its surroundings the bomb had exploded. Father Douglas
rushed out and fired his automatic at the wrong car.

We descended into the garden playground where we met
20 or so children who allowed us to take their photographs.
Then we went into the church – some of the children had
followed us and stood clustered around the door. The church
is large and airy, restful in its simple decoration, and provides
seating for about 200 worshippers. I asked Father Douglas to
pray for us. He explained the Chaldean rite in which
Aramaic, almost certainly the language that Jesus himself
would have spoken, is used. Some elements of the liturgy date

Father Douglas with children in the garden playground

back to the third century and Father Douglas, with the help of one of the lads, sang a benediction which was very moving.

Father Douglas entertained us royally with a fine spread of Iraqi dishes. He explained that hospitality was part of his duty and he objected strongly to being thanked. In his room there were two Kalashnikov style semi-automatic rifles but in the presence of such a brave man it did not seem correct to launch into a diatribe on pacifism.

After the visit to the St Mari Church we returned to the apartment building and on the following morning, Saturday 26 November, we took our places in a large people carrier which had plenty of room for Jim, Harmeet and myself as well as the driver and a translator. Greg Rollins would normally have accompanied us but Tom Fox offered to take his place to give Greg a break from delegation duties. How fateful Tom's kind offer was to prove. How would the composition of the original party have affected the outcome? With three Canadians and an Englishman. I would certainly have been at greater risk as the only representative of a Coalition nation.

The day started with an exploration of a Baghdad souk

The 'Magic Sheet'
(in English with Arabic on the reverse side)

Christian Peacemaker Teams
Greetings and Peace

Christian Peacemaker Teams (CPT) is a volunteer violence-reduction team. We work with Iraqi people for peace and human rights by building relationships and opposing injustice with creative non-violence. We respect people of all religions and ethnicities, and we do not try to change anyone's religion. CPT is a self-funded, independent group, not affiliated with a political party or government. CPT cannot provide financial or employment assistance.

Although we are glad Iraqis are free from Saddam's oppression, we oppose the US invasion and ongoing occupation.

Christian Peacemaker Teams has also worked in Palestine, Haiti, Colombia, and Mexico as well as several locations in North America. In Iraq, we:

1. Live in a local community and interact with Iraqis on a daily basis.
2. Continue to work closely with the newly formed Muslim Peacemaker Teams for an Iraqi society free from militarisation and violence.
3. Collaborate with Iraqi human rights organisations, walk with them in non-violent demonstrations, help form coalitions with other groups, and communicate their stories to our home communities.
4. Work for justice and human rights for Iraqi detainees. Please contact us if you know Iraqis who would like to

tell us about the human rights violations they've suffered at the hands of the US military, Iraqi National Guard or Iraqi Police. We will share their stories with North Americans and Europeans.

5. Pray for peace and carry out public actions for peace in Iraq and our home countries.

6. Educate people in our home countries about the situation in Iraq and encourage them to work for change.

Our work is to reduce violence around the world and is inspired by leaders such as Gandhi and his Muslim colleague Badsha Khan and peacemakers from other traditions.
Peace be with you.

North American Offices
USA: PO Box 6508, Chicago IL 60680
Phone 773 277 0253
US email: peacemakers@cpt.org

CANADA: 25 Cecil St, Unit 307; Toronto ON M5T INI
Phone 416 423 5525
Canada email: canada@cpt.org

website: http://www.cpt.org

4

THE TWO HOUSES

You see little of Baghdad from the boot of a car.
Norman Kember

The morning after our kidnap, we awoke in handcuffs on the carpeted floor in the main room – not that we had had much sleep. The two minders supervised our trips to the *hammam* and then we were moved into the second room where we sat in a row of chairs facing the wall. That is where we spent our waking hours. For the first two days in captivity we were fed on sweet biscuits – a packet was handed to us – and occasional glasses of water. Afterwards we were fed bread – diamond shaped simoons like pitta bread – with perhaps half a hamburger in them. The ends of the bread were a bit tough. I also remember being provided with an apple because I used, and kept, the stalk as a primitive toothpick.

In the evening we were brought back into the main room to sleep. The younger minder we called Junior. I don't know where he slept although there were benches round the side of the main room and Junior probably slept on a bench. The main minder, 'Uncle', who was an enormous man, never slept in a bed at all. He slept on the floor behind us.

The man we called Number One was given this name because we thought at first that he was the chief of the group. He slept in one of the two beds in the second room. In that

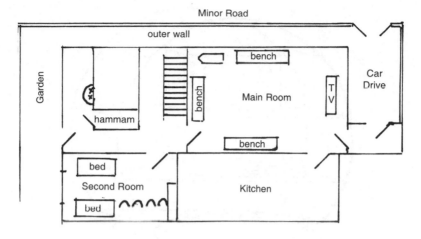

My plan of House No. 1

room there was also a coat stand and a kind of wardrobe with a dressing table set into it. There were hair brushes and other items on the dressing table but otherwise the room was bare. Number One wore Western suits and was careful in his appearance   he always cleaned his shoes.

The single window was always covered with long curtains. Across the hallway was the staircase and a door into the eastern-type toilet, a shallow ceramic basin with two raised foot rests on either side of a hole. There was a flushing system but it didn't flush. A tap with a small jug was provided for washing hands. To the left was a washbasin and then a door – perhaps to the garden. To the right was the way into the main room where we spent the night and a door into the kitchen. A radio in the kitchen was often set to a channel with extended chanting of readings from the Qur'an.

On the second night we were put down to sleep on the carpet in the main room in front of the television set, which was attached to a nearly circular vertical frame. The frame had two shelves, one for the TV set and one for the DVD player

[53]

A sketch of the TV on its stand

and satellite receiver. The TV set was switched on for news broadcasts in Arabic and I remember seeing a feature film, *Con Air*. The dialogue of this film was in English and we watched as a plane-load of convicts loosened their handcuffs prior to escape!

Our captors also showed one or two DVDs of the Mujahideen in action against American armoured vehicles and troops. The TV was often left on till after midnight but it was difficult to watch from our prone position.

Lying on our backs we had plenty of time to examine the fancy plasterwork on the ceiling, the fan and the lights. By the decoration it was evidently an older style of house. At night a small kerosene lamp was kept alight. On the walls there was a western calendar set at November and one or two pictures including a Christian one, a Sacred Heart picture of Jesus. An unusual heart-shaped clock was mounted on one wall and, bizarrely, there was an ironing board in one corner.

It was during the second night that the dog started to bark. This was a large black and brown watchdog that was proba-

bly kept in the driveway. I saw it once in the passageway leading from the kitchen to the outside. Roused by the barking,
the captors came rushing in, woke us up and accused Tom of
trying to escape. Tom was slapped and then the handcuffs
were changed so that we were shackled to each other, wrist
to wrist and the man at the end chained to a bench. It didn't
take us long to realise that Tom was the hostage our captors
liked least. We did not know it at the time but Tom had had
his US army card on him when he had been taken.

A more thorough search followed and the captors took my
belt and the pouch attached to it. Inside the pouch were my
driving license and £300 in a mixture of US dollars, Euros and
Iraqi dinars. From my driving licence our captors learned that
I was 'Doctor' Kember. Thereafter I became 'The Doctor'. Jim,
Harmeet and Tom continued to be addressed by their
Christian names. In the pouch was also a strip of beta-blocker
tablets that I took for high blood pressure. The captors took
the details and within two days I had a box full of beta-
blockers brought by Medicine Man (hence the nickname).

As the days passed, I learned to say '*Munkin Mie?*' asking
for water and '*Hammam?*' for a trip to the squat-style toilet in
the cubby hole by the stairs. At this stage I tended to make
the requests since Tom, Jim and Harmeet felt that our captors
would respect my seniority. Eventually the captors came to
think that I was a bit of a wimp. They liked Harmeet. He is
such a pleasant chap that it would have been difficult not to
like him. Tom they regarded with obvious distrust.

As we sat in manacles in the second room during the day,
Number One would come to stand behind us out of sight
(we always had to put on blindfolds when he thought he
might be seen). He liked to talk and had a good level of
English. He passed to us, while standing behind us, pictures of
members of his family, including children who had been
killed just because their car had approached too close to an

[55]

American convoy near Fallujah. He told us that with the death of these precious family members all purpose had gone out of his life. In later discussion he said that there were no real differences between Shias and Sunnis – they were all Iraqis. Differences had been exaggerated by the Coalition forces for their own ends.

Number One obviously lived in this house and it might even have belonged to him. He went off to work every day and did not take an active part in holding us. He seemed more detached than the other minders and avoided talk about the reasons why we were held or our possible fate. Later we learned that he was studying English – he was reading Marlowe's *Dr Faustus* and Ernest Hemingway's *The Old Man and the Sea*. He asked if I could help him and I responded that Harmeet was better qualified for this task because he was studying to teach English. We did not see or hear of Number One after we left this first house.

During our first two days we did hear some whimpering noises from the top of the stairs and wondered if there was another kidnap victim in the house. The sound was of someone pleading or in distress. Jim and Harmeet said that shortly after our capture a person was led out of the house during the night and past us as I slept. They felt guilty that they had raised no voice in protest.

There was another incident that must have occurred early in the week. It was evening and we were lying on the floor with our feet away from the door when we heard a woman's voice. I became aware that she was standing in the doorway. By tilting my head backwards I could see her – but upside down. She was tall by comparison with the doorway and dressed in a long black or navy-blue dress. Her head was covered but not her face. I said, 'Salaam Alaikum' ('Peace be to you'), a customary greeting. I forget if she replied.

Towards the end of our first week a new character came

[56]

on the scene who we called Video Man. Strangely, Video Man always brought his small son aged about four with him. Two videos were made on successive days. On the first one we each made a simple statement of who we were and why we were in Baghdad. We were given our passports to hold as proof of our identities and the video zoomed in on them.

For the second video two new orange jumpsuits were produced (as worn at Guantánamo Bay). Tom and I were told to wear them. I objected, saying that I was not a prisoner of war but had come in peace. But as Tom agreed to wear one, I followed his example since he was the senior CPT man. Jim and Harmeet were videoed without the suits.

We were asked to plead for release with tears but Jim argued that that would inevitably look false on the video. On a future occasion the minders wanted to ruffle my hair so that I looked more desperate but my objection that I still had some human dignity was accepted.

Medicine Man was obviously the leader of this group. He started the story during the first week that the two Canadians would be released first as a gesture of goodwill from his group of patriots. Tom and I would be released shortly afterwards.

We believed this and were reassured by the 'Canadians first' story, although our spirits fell as the date for our flights back to Amman passed on Thursday 1 December. We were quite unaware that Medicine Man's Sword of Righteousness Brigade had issued an ultimatum along with the videos. Unless all Iraqi prisoners were freed by 8 December the four of us would be killed.

I cannot recall what we talked about during that first week. I think that we spent much time wrapped in our private thoughts. We did acquire a small piece of paper, perhaps from the biscuit wrappers, and Harmeet and I tried to remember how to fold origami peace cranes. After several mis-folds we succeeded and Harmeet went on to become an expert at folding tiny cranes from the silver wrappers around the sweets that we were occasionally given.

At the end of that first week – Sunday 4 December – Tom was driven away without any real explanation. I was rewarded with the same experience later the same day – taken out of the house in handcuffs and bundled into the boot of a large car. I think that Medicine Man drove and that there was a woman sitting in the rear seat, perhaps as a decoy at check-points. The ride was 20 minutes or so. You see little of Baghdad from the boot of a car – you just feel the bumps in the road. When the car came to a stop in a driveway I was hauled unceremoniously out of the boot and propelled into the house that was to be our place of captivity for the next three and half months.

I remember being ushered into the downstairs living room and there was Tom. Uncle and another man whom we nick-named Nephew (no relation!) were also there. For the first night we slept on the floor of this room in front of the tele-vision set and I remember that late at night I heard my name being spoken on the TV. I strained to look at the set but saw no images of myself.

The next morning we were taken up the staircase to the room where we were to spend the rest of our captivity. Tom was shackled day and night by a chain to the door handle, the chain being passed round both the inner and outer handles and thus quite secure. A piece of cloth was also included in the fixture so that the chains did not rattle against the wooden door. I was handcuffed to Tom.

During the day we sat side by side in two of the ubiquitous plastic garden chairs. At night a futon was laid on the floor and we slept on it, handcuffed together. Tom at 6'2" was considerably taller than me and slept diagonally across the futon. This left me a corner space that seemed to diminish in size by the morning. Once or twice during the night we would agree to stand up for ten minutes or so to ease aching joints and relieve boredom.

Two grey pillows were provided and the stuffing was coming out of one of them. I used the apple stalk as a primitive needle and managed to stitch up the leaking end. The stuffing was a rough type of cotton wool and came in useful later in our captivity to clear up messy accidents since on only one occasion were we provided with paper tissues.

A distinguishing noise in this house was the one that at first sounded to me like the quacking of ducks. In fact it was the croaking of a species of black and white crow (perhaps hooded crows) and there were a large number of them near the house. I did see one of them dimly through the frosted glass of the *hammam*, but after the first two weeks these birds seemed to fly away from the area. Another sound was a chiming clock – a tinkle rather than a robust chime. It sounded the hours and the half hours. We listened and counted the chimes when awake during the night. This chime was turned off after two or three days although the clock was still to be seen in the hallway downstairs.

While Tom and I were alone in this house two videos were made. The first I have tried to banish from my mind – we were put into the orange suits again chained up, handcuffed, blindfolded and then made to kneel. I have since seen a recording of this captivity video – it is chilling.

The second video was quite bizarre. We were taken downstairs and seated, without handcuffs, at a small table against the wall. On the table were chocolates and an orange drink. We were told that this was to be a 'release' video and that we had to look correspondingly joyful. I think Tom and I toasted each other in orange fizz. It is doubtful whether this video was ever shown on Al Jazeera or anywhere else.

Why were we moved from one house to another? I do not know. Perhaps the first one was a clearing house. We had the feeling they hadn't had possession of House No. 2 very long and Tom and I were made to sleep downstairs with them the first night because they were preparing the room upstairs ready for our occupancy.

How did Tom and I pass the time together that first week? I do not recall very much but I know that I asked about his days as a clarinettist in the United States Marine Band and he told me he often played at formal occasions in the White House. Tom had met all the American presidents since Nixon. His band also travelled abroad and he had been to many countries in Europe. In addition to the band, he played in chamber groups and major orchestras. After 20 years he had retired and taken up work in a chain of health food stores. About this time Tom joined the Quakers. I think I must have also related a little of my life story but there was a deal of silence between us.

Tom and I continued to accept the 'Canadians first' theory of release because Medicine Man had made so much of this. We assumed that Jim and Harmeet had already been given their freedom from House No. 1 and were anticipating our own freedom by the end of the week. In fact the Canadians were exactly where we had left them with the younger minder, Junior, in attendance. Among other irritations they were suffering the continued background noise of the television to which Junior was much attached.

The room of confinement in which Tom and I found ourselves had a window that overlooked the driveway at the side of the house. For three days we listened to every sound that might mean a car was coming to take us to a place of release. None came.

On Sunday 11 December the door opened and in walked James Loney. Tom and I knew then that the promise of release was a lie. In a few hours Harmeet was also led into the room and our number was complete.

[60]

5

THE ROGUES' GALLERY

A naughty person, a wicked man, walketh with a froward [contrary] mouth, he teacheth with his fingers.

Proverbs 6:12, 13 Authorised Version

There were always two minders keeping a vigil at night but not always during the day. A period of duty seemed to be about seven days 'on' with three or four days off. At exercise time the minders would often complain of lack of sleep, so it is probable that they had turns keeping watch during the night. When Medicine Man, the leader, arrived, we would hear him talking for some time to the minders on duty before coming upstairs to present his information – misinformation – to us.

In talking to the other minders we called Medicine Man *Hadji Inglese*, 'Hadji' being a courtesy title but strictly applicable only to one who has journeyed to Mecca. He was about 5'9" and well built with a fair paunch. We suggested that he would benefit from eating the same diet as we did in order to lose weight.

Medicine Man spoke English with a limited vocabulary and did not always understand our comments or requests. When I said during one of his visits that, in effect, he had

Medicine Man, Uncle, Junior and Nephew

kidnapped not me but my wife, he did not know the word 'kidnap'!

The minders kept in constant touch with him by mobile phone. They used these devices frequently and liked to show off to us fresh images or games they had acquired. They were also proud to demonstrate new ring tones.

Medicine Man was seldom on duty as a 'minder' and never slept at the house as far as I know. He appeared promptly when there was an emergency or at intervals to talk to us. He took the later videos.

He wore a variety of well-cut suits, and was also well shod. He carried a mobile phone and we decided that he was in business in Baghdad. He claimed to have once acted as interpreter for the American forces. He also said that he was pursuing a college course. He had a daughter who was at secondary school (it was her Christian friend who later produced Jesus DVDs).

We saw him about once every ten days and occasionally twice in succession. Once there was a period of three weeks when we didn't see him and we asked 'Where's Hadji Inglese got to?' Whenever we wanted to make a request, we had to wait for Medicine Man to turn up. If you wished to be told lies direct you had to wait for him – you got them second hand from the minders.

The apparently genial **Uncle** was the minder-in-chief. He was about 40 and perhaps 6' tall. He had black hair and a black bushy moustache. He was very heavily built with enormous feet and large podgy hands. He was so heavy that he caused the top of the wooden box we used as a table to cave in when he sat on it, and also broke a small metal chair. Among the oddments on the floor in our captivity room there was a glass bowl which formed part of a ceiling lamp, and in trying to sound it like a gong Uncle broke it with his fist and spread glass everywhere. We had the job of clearing up the widely dispersed fragments. He spoke little English but used his hands to express himself e.g. to indicate bad smells or to keep us quiet. He had three distinct hand signals – he would place his two forefingers side by side and then slide one against the other saying 'Shia, Americky', meaning that the Americans and the Shias were hand in glove. Uncle was strongly anti-Shia! Another signal was to rub his thumb against the forefinger saying 'no hubus' ('no bread' i.e. no ransom money!), followed by the rising movement with the other hand as if to show an aircraft taking off (no release).

During one of the video sessions he lifted me up by the lapels and stood me against the wall. He was duly admonished by Medicine Man for this act of discourtesy to an old man.

Uncle was interested in the Canadians and particularly in cowboys. He tried to mime questions to Jim and Harmeet about living conditions in Canada. He drew a picture of his

Uncle's sketch of his house as drawn in Jim's notebook (see p. 90)

house in one of the books and I responded with a drawing of mine. I do not remember him talking at any time about a family.

His outfit was invariably a shell suit in dark blue or grey – one of them had the word 'Gamma' on it. He always wore plastic slip-on sandals on his enormous feet. Occasionally Uncle appeared in the morning in his baggy underpants with a black and white checked pattern. He only appeared briefly in outdoor clothes and I have no clear recollection of what he wore then. Like the other minders, he carried a cigarette lighter and a mobile phone with a blue light. I recall that he occasionally played with 'worry' beads. He always slept on the floor and kept a pistol under his pillow.

We felt that Uncle was a countryman. He certainly had rough manners and happily spat anywhere on the stone floor. One day he brought us in a fragrant rose and then later another flower from the garden and we talked (or gestured) to him about gardens and farming. We believed he had been in the army during the Iraq-Iran conflict and he may have been a cook. Later he must have been active with the insurgents as he showed us a watch with a khaki strap which he claimed to have taken from a dead American soldier.

Uncle was at least as bored as we were and roamed the various rooms in the house sorting through the goods that the previous occupiers had left there, probably looking for items to sell. He took a football from our room but subsequently twisted his ankle badly when playing in a game.

He would bring various items he had found around the house and ask us where they had been made. One object was an army self heating pouch, probably designed to be wrapped around a tin of soup or drink. We tried to explain the instructions and Uncle could not be restrained from adding water to the chemicals – and discovering that the system did indeed work. There were numerous tubes of cosmetic creams in a cabinet downstairs. One tube contained a lubricant for sexual intercourse and we were able to convey to him the purpose for which it was designed. He later came back and mimed that he had persuaded Nephew to use it as a hair cream – much mirth.

Junior was between 25 and 30 years old, 5'10" to 6' tall, lithe and not overweight as the others were. He had many pockmarks on his face and occasionally smoked.

Junior spoke a few words in English, mainly commands like 'sit down' and 'sleep'. His teeth were very prominent in a wide mouth under a thin moustache. He claimed to have been wounded by shrapnel in his shoulder and leg but I did not see the scars. A scar on his scalp was slightly visible when he pointed it out to us.

He, too, wore a shell suit when in the house – blue with a stripe down the arms and the trouser legs. He went out smartly dressed in a variety of colourful shirts, worn under a jacket when it was cold. Junior's outdoor shoes had long square toes and I think he fancied himself as a smart dresser.

We think he may have been a taxi driver. In the evening we could hear his car being driven up beside the house while in the morning he would allow the engine to tick over for 20 minutes before driving away.

He told us that he had lost many of his close family in the Coalition attack on Fallujah at the end of 2004. He asked Jim, 'If the Americans invaded your country, would you not become a mujahideen?' Junior's moods varied from day to day. He was excitable and more unreliable than the others. He would get impatient if I was slow to get back into my seat or lie down at night. He even threatened one day to stop me going to the *hammam* until Nephew reasoned with him. Junior almost exploded when I placed a shod foot on a chair to tie up the lace. He shoved me away – '*Harran!*' – it was a seat that the minders used. He would appear at night, creeping silently up the felted steps to check that we were not up to any forbidden activity. We had the impression that Nephew and Junior did not get on well together, perhaps because Junior was so brash in his speech and manners.

Jim told us about an event that happened during the week while Harmeet and he were alone under Junior's care in House No. 1. They were in the main room and Junior was cleaning his pistol when he fired it accidentally. The gun must have been pointing upwards because a large hole appeared in the ceiling plaster. Junior rushed about to clear up the mess on the carpet, hoping perhaps that his blunder would go unnoticed.

Nephew (I don't know who dreamt up the nicknames – they just arose) was perhaps the oldest at about 45. He was about 5'9" and rather overweight with a paunch. Nephew tried to speak some English and had a larger vocabulary than Uncle or Junior, but was not fluent. He was married with children and we understood that he had lost his house in Fallujah and was living with his family in the home of a relative. He often appeared to be in a depressed state, probably seeing no future for himself or his children. He wore a shell suit decorated with lettering in English down each arm – something about a beach competition in the USA. We did not see him in outdoor clothes.

We assumed that he lived nearby since he occasionally came in with food – a spicy dish cooked by his wife. He was more uncomfortable than the other two with his role as keeper of captives and often apologised for locking us up. But in spite of this he was careful to do his invigilation duties properly. I remember the occasion when he produced a new automatic pistol that he had just bought, showing it to us as if to prove how macho he was. But when he was by himself in the house he would call downstairs or whistle to a pretend companion!

The minders varied in their religious practice. In the later days when we made regular trips into their room downstairs I cannot recall Uncle ever engaged in devotions while Nephew did pray from time to time. Junior was regular in his use of the prayer mat and often read from the Qur'an. He was most fervent in his devotions, praying with tears when his sister was ill.

The prayer mat had a picture of a mosque in blue on a grey background. Sometimes the radio was tuned in to a recital of the Qur'an and on one day – it was a festival – Junior came into our room, lit a joss stick and, much to Jim's displeasure, wedged it into a hole in the wall.

6

A ROOM WITH NO VIEW

*I know a great deal about 150 square feet of Iraq
– but otherwise very little.*

Norman Kember

My rough sketch shows the view we had each day as we sat
against the wall facing the window. Furniture, mainly chairs,
was piled up under the window which was covered over one
half with a green-greyish curtain with brown symbols on it
that reminded me of chromosomes. The other half was hung
with a lighter material – perhaps a sheet which was marked
with stains. This meant that we lived in semi-darkness.

Only when the window was opened to let in some fresh
air did we see the sunlight on the high wall opposite.
Occasionally we saw the shadow of a tree moving on this
wall. The window had decorative but strong steel bars beyond
the glass. The bars were painted in a light green colour –
eau-de-Nil?

At some time in the past it appeared that water had leaked
through the ceiling because there were strips of paper hanging down from the ceiling and on the walls. The left wall from
where we sat was painted a pinkish colour and the other walls
grey or green/grey. The floor was covered in stone composition tiles – white with flecks of black and about ten inches

Captive's eye view of our room in House No. 2

square. Our room was just over twelve tiles in breadth and perhaps sixteen in length and these tiles were used for flooring in rooms and passages throughout the house.

The drawing shows the piled up chairs on which we hung clothes that we were not wearing – there were a few plastic clothes hangers. We kept our pillows and other bedding at this end of the room during the day. There were many other items there, including a very ornate carved chair in the corner and a large bell-shaped aluminium shade for a spotlight – perhaps it had been used to illuminate parties held on the flat roof space on the upper floor. Then there were boxes that contained two darkroom clocks and a Kodak Instamatic camera. Uncle used the Instamatic box to make a shade for a ceiling lamp so that no light from the bulb fell on the window. A second fitting in the ceiling near the window had a glass bowl shade but never provided any illumination.

There was a football and a long box, the contents of which

we could not see until Uncle came into our room on one of his forays. Inside the box were the components of a fluorescent light fitting which later appeared in use downstairs – Uncle was a dab hand at do-it-yourself. There was also a collection of broken tiles. On the floor was a small black wooden box studded with brass-headed nails in a decorative pattern, which Harmeet wanted to take away with him to add to his collection of other souvenirs. I seem to recall that he had had problems bringing a piece of decorative driftwood through New Zealand customs.

Also on the floor was an octagonal lidless tin box that had once held Quality Street chocolates, which we used as a waste bin. To the right there was a hostess trolley with the original pyrex dishes still in their wrapping under the sliding top and various utensils in the cupboards of the trolley. On the left there was a roughly 2.5 feet square wooden box covered in soft grey material on the sides. It had probably contained big old-fashioned loudspeakers. The wooden box was an important item of furniture as we used it as a table for eating and for playing games.

The sketch does not show the mosquitoes. They joined us at night. Fortunately they were more annoying aurally than in their bites. We pulled our woolly caps down over our ears to keep out the buzzing and they found landing sites on our faces or hands. A bite on the hands could itch for a few hours. I wrote some doggerel about the mosquitoes:

A mosquito explores the space around my head.
Will God provide for him his daily bread?
It is no surprise, a random slap –
the creature survives my blind attack.
But advantage changes come the dawn
The evidence – my blood-stained palm.

I usually had the advantage of being at the end of the row and having my left hand free so that I could attempt to swat them at night. In the morning there was an occasional mosquito to be seen on the walls. It required a deft blow with the flat of the hand to dispatch it but a red blot on the wall indicated success in killing a mosquito that had made a meal on one of us. By the time we left there must have been 30 such blots on the walls behind and beside our sleeping area. The minders had a spray that they used downstairs but Jim objected to the chemical pollution when they used it in our room. Once they brought up a mosquito coil and lit that in an attempt to keep the mosquitoes at bay.

When it got very cold in December and January a *suba* – a kerosene-powered heater – was sometimes brought in. The *suba* had a radiant heating coil and a simple hot plate on the top that could be used for boiling water or heating food. Often the minders complained that there was not enough kerosene to fill our *suba*. They blamed George Bush the robber ('Bush Ali Baba')! They always had their own *suba* burning whenever we went downstairs.

One source of body chilling was the draught that seemed to flow along the wall where we sat. We used a very thick double pile blanket to cover our legs and laps while we kept on all the clothes we had to avoid shivering.

It was perhaps in late January that Uncle brought a three-bar electric fire into our room and thrust the bare wires into a socket on the wall. In spite of this primitive electrical connection the fire came on and provided heat for us – when there was an electricity supply. The red glow from the fire at times when power was on at night was something of a comfort. At the end of one bar there was occasional sparking, which worried Jim.

If this description sounds boring, then it conveys something of our boredom of looking at little else for three months.

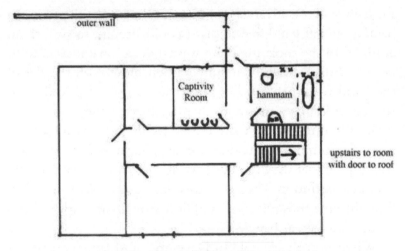

My plan of the first floor of House No. 2

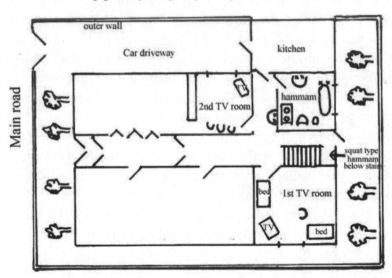

My plan of the ground floor of House No. 2

Across the small corridor from our room was the *hammam* with two batman stickers on the top of the door – an indication that children had lived in the house. This bathroom had a blue washbasin (Armitage/Shanks) covered in extensive

[72]

limescale deposits and a matching western-style toilet that did not flush (we used a large plastic jug for flushing). The sides of the toilet pan were decorated with the remnants of ancient faeces. There was a broken yellow plastic seat which could be balanced on the pan if you wished to avoid contact with the chilly ceramic. There was also a white bath with a shower and two taps on the wall that might have supplied a bidet.

Hanging from the redundant shower fitting over the bath was a macramé string bag with a number of partly used bars of toilet soap in it. These were later pressed into use after rough attempts to clean accumulated dirt and grit from their surfaces. The shower curtain had long since disintegrated but the rail proved useful for drying clothes.

The waste pipe on the sink leaked and the water that overflowed onto the floor was squeegeed into a central drain by the bath. From time to time there was a blockage in the sink waste and I fear that Harmeet's long hair was a contributory factor.

Above the bath were two small windows with square-patterned frosted glass. These were secured by Junior after Tom was accused of trying to escape through them even though there were bars on the outside.

How do you go to the toilet when you are handcuffed in a line? Simple: you are released one by one at the morning exercise time. You cross the passage, put on the plastic *hammam* slippers and enter the bathroom.

Downstairs there was another bathroom which had a peach-coloured toilet suite including a bidet. We used this once for a wash-down. Later on, we were taken on evening trips downstairs to watch the television and used a small eastern squat-type *hammam* in a tiny cupboard-like room under the stairs. Squat-type toilets have a rubber or flexible hose for washing your rear end. Since there is no toilet paper you rapidly learn why the right hand alone is used for eating as

[73]

the left hand is unclean. You also learn to keep the nails on the left hand short and a pair of nail clippers were provided from time to time.

In emergencies upstairs we were supposed to make a loud knocking sound on our door and a minder would come up to unlock the person taken short. They did not always come promptly. At night we would use a plastic drinks bottle which we kept for the purpose – the *hammam* bottle. In order to avoid accidents you had to disturb the others so that you could move away from the sleeping area to use the bottle while handcuffed. Since my digestive system did not settle into a regular pattern in all the time in captivity I had two or three other emergencies. Three or four times a day we did a 'stand up' to stretch our legs but when I was expecting some bowel movement I would remain sitting to keep control. Since it was only at one end of the line that we were chained to a fixture, the door handle, it was possible for me at the free end to get to the toilet while the others stretched out across the passageway. But it was embarrassing. Even more embarrassing was the time when I was forced to use one of the dishes from the hostess trolley as a potty.

The captors always respected our privacy in the *hammam*, although they did call out if we took too long during the morning break. I also remember that during one of our infrequent wash-down bath sessions I came out of the bathroom naked to collect some pants. The captors quickly turned their backs in embarrassment.

Our exercise area upstairs was roughly L-shaped, with the small corridor outside our room as the horizontal limb of the L, measuring perhaps 8 by 10 feet. Along that corridor and to the left was a door into a room that overlooked the driveway.

The passage in the centre of our floor was the down stroke of the L. This passage was about 10 by 20 feet and from it three doors opened onto other rooms on the floor. The stairs from below came up at one end of the passage and continued upwards to the top floor which had a small covered area leading to a door onto what we surmised was a flat roof.

The stairs were concrete with open treads. The flight coming upwards was covered in rubbish-strewn brown felt, but the second flight, to the upper floor, was of bare concrete. On each set of stairs there was a landing with a large window but the view was obscured with frosted glass or a curtain and there were metal bars beyond the glass.

Once when the window on the upper landing was opened to let in fresh air I did manage to look out and see a little of the garden with its high wall and a few roof tops beyond.

Except on rare occasions, we were roused between 9.00 and 10.00 am, when one of the minders came up to release us from the handcuffs and chains. If it was Uncle, he would hold his hand to his nose and cross the room to open the window a little to let in fresh air. When Uncle was due to have his few days off he would tend to get us up early so that he could get away and that made the rest of that day very long. Once on our feet, the first customer went off to the *hammam* – 'Anyone desperate?'

Time in the *hammam* was spent on washing and cleaning teeth (after the toothbrushes arrived) with perhaps a little clothes washing – underpants, socks or a shirt which were hung to dry on the rail of the shower curtain or on the banister of the stairs. Tom practised a two-minute complete wash-down. Then there were chores like emptying the *hammam* bottle, filling the two water bottles (all these were standard 1.4 litre lemonade bottles but with distinguishing labels!) and washing up the stainless steel beakers. The aim was to spend as much time as you could without raising the ire of the minder, who would call out if anyone took too long. The minders never came into the bathroom while we were in there.

[75]

While we went in turn to the *hammam*, the others folded up the bedclothes, lifted the futon, folded it up and swept beneath it. The chairs were then put in place against the wall and a small piece of carpet and one of the scruffier pillows were set out as foot rests. This was the time to fetch changes of clothes from their place on the pile of furniture or any medicines from the top of the hostess trolley where we kept them. A minder sat at the top of the staircase to keep a watchful eye on us. Junior was particularly vigilant lest we tried to open one of the other doors and look into forbidden rooms. If any door was open even a crack he would hurry to shut it tight.

On the two occasions when I was able push open a door to take a look I found empty rooms with piles of furniture and bric-a-brac in the corners. All the windows were well barred. One room had a window sticker for an oil company – more evidence that children had been living in the house at one time. There was absolutely nothing significant to see. I do not know why Junior was so touchy, unless he thought we were 'casing the joint' for escape.

Exercise time was precious. Each of us had our own pattern of exercises. Tom preferred to do his – various muscle and joint extension exercises he had learned at yoga classes – in the quiet of our room. Jim had a range of stretching positions designed to keep muscles supple. He exercised vigorously and included press-ups in his routine. Harmeet used to run up and down the stairs when he felt that he was in good condition. Sometimes he would wake up and say, 'I haven't got the energy this morning'. He also did press-ups. Harmeet was keen to add chin-ups to his repertoire but his attempt to hang from the top of our door resulted in dirty hands and a suspicious protest from the minder.

I spent most of my time walking briskly in a rectangular circuit around the edge of the passage, doing some step aerobics on the first of the stair treads or occasionally walking up the stairs to the next landing. I did a few basic movements in an effort to keep my pelvis and lower back supple. I also tried to touch my toes – a few more weeks in captivity and I might have made it ...

The periods of exercise had another valuable function. If we had issues that we wished to raise confidentially about one of the others, then when that person was in the toilet we could talk freely about them. This was not a common practice but on occasion it did relieve tensions. To take a trivial example, Harmeet insisted that with our request for books, the Bible and/or the Qur'an, we include an English Dictionary. I told Jim, in Harmeet's absence, that I thought that this additional request would put the main demand in jeopardy. More significantly, when Tom was washing in the bathroom one of us said, 'Did Tom really say that he had had his US Army card on him when we were kidnapped?' I wonder what they discussed in my absence?

When Junior was on duty he invariably joined in the exercises and would sometimes annoy me by doing shadow boxing into my face. I tried to mime that in my youth I had been a cross-country runner and a rock climber – more of a rock scrambler perhaps. Nephew would also do exercises when he was not depressed.

After this period for personal hygiene and exercise we were ushered back into the room and sat down on the row of chairs: two standard garden-type plastic chairs with arms alternating with two dining room chairs without arms. I used some fabric to cushion the back of my seat and the minders grew restive if I was slow at arranging it. We were then handcuffed and Tom, or whoever was seated at the right end of the chairs, was chained to the door.

Breakfast came up at about 11.00 am and after that we were left on our own until 2.00 or 3.00 pm, when the next batch of food appeared and we were released in turn for the *hammam*. Although we had had our exercise period in the morning Tom felt it important to keep exercising during the day and from time to time we would all stand up and then start walking or running on the spot for five to ten minutes. We also did a stretching exercise – raising our handcuffed hands above our heads. I irreverently called this 'armpits to the Lord' after the fashion of charismatic prayer. The last meal came between 7.00 and 9.00 pm. How we kept ourselves occupied in the intervals between meals is the subject of a later chapter.

When Nephew was on duty Harmeet always spent time with him, asking if there was any news. With Nephew it was always good news – release shortly. I knew that this misinformation came from Medicine Man and took no part in subsequent speculations between the others on the possible outcome.

In the evening we were either sitting in our row against the wall or, later on, downstairs watching the television. At around 10.00 pm we would be ready for sleeping. If we were downstairs we occasionally used the eastern squat-style *hammam* under the staircase and the washbasin in the hallway to clean our teeth but generally we used the upstairs bathroom for these functions.

The evening routine was the reverse of the morning – first the chairs would be stacked and then the floor area swept clean with the hand broom. When we were still all four together, the futon was laid down and then a quilted pad folded over to take up the remaining space along this wall. The other materials, curtains and so on were then laid at the bottom of the futon and finally there was a row of old pillows for our feet, since the futon was less than full body length. The four pillows in use for our heads were then brought from the chairs stacked by the window.

Next the large blanket was collected from its place on the staircase where it was put for airing. It would be spread out, making sure that it was going to cover Harmeet, Jim and myself. Tom insisted on arranging his odd collection of bed-clothes himself. These consisted of various pieces of furnishing material that the minders had found on their expeditions into other rooms in the house and – strangest of all – a white brocade wedding gown! Near the end of our captivity we were provided with floral sheets and pillowcases to cover the far-from-clean futon and pillows.

Medicines were collected from their box on the hostess trolley and water bottles were placed next to the door for Tom and beside me for the rest of us. If the electric fire was in use we positioned it so that it would not toast any toes during the night. At this stage we were very occasionally given a bag of dates for distribution. We preferred to eat these before lying down to avoid having date stones in the bed.

All this was done under the eye of one of the minders with either the electric lamp, a storm lantern or the blue mobile phone lights for illumination. The lantern slowly clouded up with a deposit of carbon on the inside of the glass. Uncle cleaned this off from time to time using the cloth that hung on our door to keep the chain from rattling. Jim found that the carbon layer could be removed more easily with a damp cloth.

Light in the *hammam* was provided by a further lantern, a small candle or a circular ceiling fluorescent light if the power had sufficient voltage. If the voltage was low this fluorescent tube might flicker annoyingly and you could see it out of the corner of your eye from our room for an hour or so.

When everybody had done everything, Tom, or the person by the door, was chained up by the wrist and a small piece of carpet with a cloth was placed under the door to reduce draughts and muffle the chain noise. My right ankle was chained to Tom's left ankle. The linking handcuffs were put on.

We generally persuaded the minder to put the handcuffs on more loosely at night than during the day and to leave sufficient slack on the chains to allow some movement during sleep. It was possible to rest on one's side for brief periods with one arm twisted awkwardly behind the back – again, with the permission of one's neighbours.

I developed a method of wrapping a piece of cloth round my right ankle, hidden under the sock, to ease the friction of the chain at night. While there were four of us, I always slept on the small quilted pad and perhaps it was the curvature of the pad that brought on considerable back and pelvic pains by the morning. I generally slept next to Jim and he would kindly allow me to disturb him, place my pillow vertically and sit against the wall for ten or fifteen minutes early in the morning. I also suffered from sore skin on my right thigh and so had difficulty sleeping for long on my right side. I had the squirrel-like habit of storing food to eat later. I invariably kept back a little bread and put it in my top jacket pocket to eat at night and stave off stomach pains.

Finally the lantern was moved into the hall way. A check was made that the light switch was off so that we would not be disturbed in the night should the power come on, the door was closed as far as the chain would allow and the minders left us alone. We could hear the television set well into the night. When Junior was on duty we could also hear his loud voice, often seemingly in dispute with the others. We got on with the business of trying to sleep and endeavoured not to disturb the others – unless one of us needed to go to the *hammam* in the middle of the night.

7

MENU AT THE KIDNAP KAFÉ

Choice of beverages: tap water (with a dash of sus-
pended sand particles after storms).
Norman Kember

For the first month we stayed in the clothes we were wearing
when we were kidnapped. In the end the smell got to the
kidnappers and we were provided with vest, pants, socks, a
sweater and tracksuit trousers. My trousers were Cambridge
blue, very baggy and far too long. I had to roll them up at the
bottoms to prevent them getting wet from the soggy *hammam*
floor. One day, after Christmas, Medicine Man came with
four pairs of shoes – ready, he said, for our release. These were
cheap canvas-top plimsolls with white rubber soles. The laces
provided were all either too long or too short. They arrived
in a range of sizes, all too small and particularly too small for
Tom. It was in the ribbed sole of one of these shoes that we
found the small nail. Harmeet put this nail in a pocket in one
pair of trousers and forgot about it for some weeks.

At the same time as we were given this change of clothes
we were taken in turn into the downstairs bathroom and
given a large aluminium dish of hot water with a small jug to
give ourselves a scrub down. This was the bathroom that
had a peach-coloured suite including a bidet. On this first

occasion there was some shampoo. Standing in the bath, I discovered that after a good soaping and rinsing the body starts to yield up a thick layer of accumulated dry skin that has to be rubbed off with the hands. I could have done with a strigil – the small curved metal tool used in the Roman baths to scrape off dirt and dead skin.

No towels were ever provided. Excess water was smoothed off with the hands and the body dried by the change of clothes. In the cold of winter I wore a vest, shirt, Marks and Spencer brown cardigan, sweater and jacket – the clothes in which I had arrived! When the weather warmed up I dispensed with the jacket and sweater and kept them on top of the pile of chairs by the window.

Early in January we were provided with aluminium bowls of hot water – this time with a little soap powder – to wash discarded underwear and shirts. When the powder was used up no more appeared and washing had to be done without powder, only soap.

Under Jim's guidance a good soak and a rub left the articles fairly clean. They were spread out to dry on the banisters of the staircase leading from our landing to the upper floor. This gave us the opportunity to examine furtively the door to the roof space. It was firmly locked. In the winter the clothes took two days to dry. Later washing was done by Harmeet using the twin tub washing machine that was in the downstairs bathroom, but this only worked when the electricity supply was on, so Uncle would come upstairs and make us sort out our clothes for washing in a hurry before the power failed. The cold water wash took out little of the dirt but the spin was effective and the clothes dried quickly.

After one month and some repeated requests from Jim, four toothbrushes, in distinguishing colours, were provided, plus toothpaste. Oh, the joy of cleaning your teeth for the first time after one brushless month! The first tube of paste was

Sensodyne (the labelling was invariably in Arabic and English) and I favoured this since I lost some fillings during the captivity and considered that Sensodyne might stave off toothache. Further tubes had to be requested several days in advance if we were to keep a continuous supply. I was able to press Sensodyne out of its tube for one week after the others had given up on it. They were amused by my daily reports of a fresh quarter-inch blob on my toothbrush, but for me it was a major victory when victories were in short supply! At the beginning of March Jim asked for some combs but only one ever materialised. I suspect it was thought that we would share it between us, but in the event it was decided to give it to Harmeet for his sole use since he had the greatest problems with his long hair.

We all had beards by this time. Our captors originally produced disposable razors which were quite useless without water and shaving cream. An ancient electric razor reduced the size of my beard but the others were allowed the use, under supervision, of a small pair of scissors to keep their beards in trim. On request nail clippers were provided for hands and feet. Harmeet helped me to cut my toe nails and generally looked after me – he took care that I remembered to swallow my daily blood pressure pill.

Later body wash-downs were done in the upstairs bathroom, again while standing in the bath. The water was heated in a basin by standing it on top of the *suba*. There was room for this heater on a flat surface at one end of the bath. If the water was too hot it was necessary to half fill the small jug with cold water and fill up with hot. The radiant heat of the suba was available to try to dry off the body or at least keep it warm after the wash-down. The captors were always concerned that Harmeet's hair dried properly and either brought in the *suba* or put on the electric fire for this purpose.

During January a gecko came up the waste pipe to live in the bath. He was the nearest we got to a pet but when Uncle thought it time for us to have a wash-down he killed the creature and showed us the corpse before disposing of it.

Food was a major topic but in general there was no point in getting the salivary glands excited before the meals appeared. I was the only one who didn't complain regularly about the inadequate and unbalanced diet. I had a smaller appetite and often handed on the remains of bread to others. But I was miserly and never passed on the protein-based contents.

It was possible that the minders were given an allowance for food and spent much of it on feeding themselves, although their diet was similar to ours in quality if not in quantity. Lack of food was generally a topic on the list when Medicine Man appeared. Perhaps a little more was provided after such complaints, but bread and chips remained the mainstay of our diet. We learned under Tom's tutorship that Iraqis never deny a request. Politeness demands that they always say yes, but they often fail in delivery.

Food invariably came with bread – *hubus*. This came in the form of half a 12-inch round flat bread, or diamond shaped *simoons* used like pitta bread. Very occasionally a soft roll would appear.

A Kidnap Kafé menu would run:

Breakfast
Chosen for you: bread and portion of cheese *or* fried egg *or* eggplant

Lunch
Chosen for you: bread and three, four or five chips
Today's special alternatives: fried slices of frank-

furter *or* boiled rice
Vegetable: tomato *or* raw carrot (on demand)

Dinner
Hors-d'oeuvre: choice of nothing *or* nothing
Main course, chosen for you: bread and three,
four or five chips
Today's special alternatives: fried slices of frank-
furter *or* boiled rice
Vegetable: tomato *or* raw carrot (on demand)
Dessert: occasionally dates
Beverages: tap water (with a dash of suspended
sand particles after storms)

Normally food was handed out as we sat in the row against
the wall. If it arrived during exercise, Jim tried to ensure that
breakfast food was put on a clean surface on the hostess
trolley before it was distributed. We said '*Shukran*' ('thank
you') after receiving it and perhaps '*Zaine*' ('good') if it was
something more solid, like the rarely-provided half a
hamburger.

On some occasions, normally in the early afternoon, we
would have a 'formal' meal. The minder would bring up a
large round aluminium tray with a dish of food and some
form of bread. This would be put on the grey box 'table' in
front of us and the handcuffs would be released so that we
could eat with our right hands, as it is considered unclean
(*harran*) to eat with the left hand.

We would move the chairs so that we sat one on each side
of the grey box. I might reach for the water bottle and pour
it into the two metallic beakers we mostly shared for drinking (except when Jim was ill and he insisted on keeping his
beaker separate to reduce the possibility of cross infection).

The minder sat on a seat behind us and we would

sometimes use the Arabic grace that the captors taught us *'Bismillah Al-Rahman Al-Raheem'* ('In the name of Allah, most gracious, most merciful'). If someone had an urgent call to the toilet we would wait for them to return before starting to eat.

If the dish contained rice there would be spoons provided, but normally we were expected to eat using the bread to scoop up the chips or sliced frankfurter and tomato or whatever was provided. One hazard was conveying the food from the bowl to the mouth without spilling it. I used my plastic covered notebook as a table mat so that any spillages could be consumed from its surface. Rice invariably came without any flavouring and was the hardest to eat if there were no spoons and we had to spend time picking up odd grains from the floor after a meal. We were afraid that the small ants that lived on the floor in the *hammam* might be attracted into our room. Pieces of food dropped on the floor were picked up (there was a five-second-rule) and eaten or not depending on the eater. Harmeet and I were not too fussy.

The minder would sometimes keep an eye on me to make sure that I ate enough, or not too much of the wrong foods that might cause toilet emergencies. It was after one of these meals that Jim admonished Harmeet and me for eating too quickly so that Tom did not receive a fair share. After this we tried to divide the food equally into quarters before starting to eat. The minders found this process amusing.

They must have bought the food in batches – we would have several days of rice and then a period of frankfurter sausages, generally sliced, and then a few days of eggplant. Chips were standard fare and most food was fried – we could hear and smell the sizzling downstairs. Occasionally we had half a hamburger. The food that was wrapped in the *hubus* or laid in the *simoon* was often greasy or had tomato juice on it. Again, the problem was to convey these items to the mouth without spilling them. If the wrap leaked, the liquid landed upon your lap. My light blue trousers were covered in grease and tomato stains and the various washing procedures never had enough cleaning power to remove them. Again, I learned to use my note book with its plastic cover as a napkin, but still some juices escaped to add to the random pattern of staining.

Rare items were chicken livers, a half chicken and a very spicy meat dish brought in by Nephew which, to my embarrassment, passed straight through me. For a few days, on Medicine Man's directive, we had milk made up with hot water from powder. I regarded this as a good breakfast food if the bread was dipped in it. But the others complained and no further packets of dried milk appeared. I drew a picture of a cow in my notebook and discovered that the word for milk was *halib*. Dates were supplied from time to time, once as a sticky block but more generally as 30 or 40 very dry fruit in a plastic bag. As I mentioned earlier, they were a treat when handed out at bedtime.

We asked for carrots as a source of fibre and had raw carrots for about three weeks. Then they brought up a large bunch but these had some remnants of earth on them. Jim insisted that we washed them thoroughly but the wet carrots quickly became inedible. Apples and halved oranges appeared now and then, and on two occasions Uncle came up with a jug of freshly squeezed orange juice – oranges grew in the garden.

How to discover the Arabic for 'milk' (halib)

Later, when we were taken downstairs in the evening, we were seated around a bowl on the floor and ate Iraqi fashion. The minders generally sat out of sight with a considerably larger quantity of food, although they occasionally passed leftovers on to us. This annoyed Jim. On one occasion the soft rolls they provided had mould on them. Harmeet, again to Jim's displeasure, was prepared to eat them. For Harmeet food was food. Stale bread could be made more palatable by heating it on the *suba* or on the top of the electric fire. We even used this fire to heat water for tea on the one occasion when they left the kettle with us.

Our drink was water from the tap in the bathroom. Tea was sometimes provided upstairs and it was generally available whenever we were downstairs. It was made with tea leaves in a battered old kettle. Sugar was spooned liberally into the drinking beakers and the tea was poured in and stirred. Because I was considered too old to handle a hot metal beaker I was provided with a china mug. This had a picture of the children's cartoon character Wile E. Coyote on the outside. It is my greatest regret that in the urgency of release I forgot to pick up the Wile E. Coyote mug!

The minders often drank fizzy drinks like 7Up and rarely offered us any. Since I was producing generous amounts of gas myself, I avoided these fizzy drinks when they were offered.

Christmas lunch, I remember, was plain boiled rice stuffed in a *simoon*. But there were also special treats. A day or two after Christmas Nephew brought in a Christmas cake. It was a chocolate sponge covered in soft icing with Christmas symbols to decorate the top. Uncle came up and cut it with his pocket knife. We had two or three pieces each and Uncle, in his usual countryman's manner, gobbled down much of the remainder. I recall that, on request, we sang a verse or two of a Christmas carol for them.

When Medicine Man came he occasionally brought

wrapped toffees or other sweets or even popcorn. Uncle liked to eat the kernels of melon seeds and would arrive with a paper bag full of seeds and distribute some to us. I found them hard to crack open and the tiny kernels not worth the bother. Uncle's discarded seed cases were to be found all over the house. In the last two weeks Nephew brought in some squares of Turkish delight with nuts in it – something like nougat.

Since it was Harmeet's birthday on 24 March we were going to suggest that Nephew produced a cake for him. In the event Harmeet had an infinitely superior birthday present!

8

HOLDING IT TOGETHER

'When I get back to Pinner!' Had I said those words? Yes, I had. They meant that there was still hope and resilience within me.

Norman Kember

My sketch of our house in Pinner

Dramatis Personae:

James Loney – Delegation Leader. CPT Organiser in Canada. Age 41. Roman Catholic.

Tom Fox – CPT full-timer in Iraq. USA. Age 54. Quaker
Harmeet Singh Sooden – Delegation Member. Canadian citizen
but lives in New Zealand. Age 32. Sikh background.
Norman Kember – Delegation Member. United Kingdom. Age
74. Baptist.

Four people who have only known each other for six days,
then find themselves shackled together for three-and-a-half
months – how do they pass the time without getting on one
another's nerves?

One way to avoid boredom is to agree a routine. When the
four of us were together in the second house we adopted a
timetable of worship and Bible study each day. For services of
worship this was a congregation of four linked in a very close
fellowship and, unlike many churches I know, all sitting
together in the front pew. This session was led in rotation but
using our own patterns of devotion. Tom and Harmeet used
the Quaker pattern of silence and waiting for Spirit-led
spoken contributions of thought. In fact Harmeet had experience of Anglican worship at his preparatory and public
schools in England. When Jim led he always included music
and spoken prayers. Tom and Jim both had a large reservoir of
sing-a-long songs they had learned and enjoyed at young
people's camps such as:

Go now in peace,
go now in peace,
let the love of God surround you,
everywhere,
everywhere you may go.

Tom taught us a song composed by Russian children which
we came to call 'Tom's song'.

If all the people lived their lives
as if it were a song into the light,
providing music for the stars
to dance their circles in the night.

We also sang some chants from the French Taizé community such as 'Laudate Dominum' ('Praise the Lord') or 'Lord, hear my prayer'. We even launched into singing these simple songs as rounds, generally with Jim and Harmeet taking one part and Tom and myself the other. We failed in an attempt to write our own song based on the phrase 'Be still'. 'Amazing Grace' was a hymn which we all knew, and our prayers some-times included the Lord's Prayer.

When it was my turn to lead I tried to follow a Baptist order of worship and started with a verse or two of a tradi-tional hymn, prayers of praise, of confession and of intercession and a reflection on a Bible passage. Initially I tried to recon-struct, in outline, an entire book of the Bible for worship starting from Genesis and going through to Revelation (with notable omissions for some of the minor prophets and Paul's letters). For Bible study we tried to recall a text or a biblical passage and this was generally discussed in four sections as suggested by Tom:

1. What does the passage say to you immediately?
2. Does the passage reflect your experience of life?
3. Are there difficulties in interpretation?
4. How will its message affect your life?

I remember putting forward difficult passages for pacifists such as Paul's insistence in his letter to the church at Rome (Romans 13:1) that Christians should always obey those in government because our rulers are appointed by God to keep order (including Blair and Bush?). To such studies we each brought our own point of view and Tom was well versed in the thought of the French historian and philosopher René Girard and his development of the idea of scapegoating. I can recommend Bible study without Bibles as you can readily invent or adapt any text you require!

I suggested that, at least in our prayer, we did not consider ourselves confined to this small room but looked on the walls as windows to the wider world. Thus the left hand wall could represent all who were captives, detained in Iraq or elsewhere for whatever reason. The wall opposite us, with the window, could give out onto the whole of creation. The right hand wall we 'filled' with all who worked for peace both in the organisations we knew and with people involved in seeking justice through fairer trade and debt relief. The wall behind us was a 'window' to those who backed us through prayer. We knew that our family and friends would be working and praying for our release in addition to a wide fellowship of churches. We had no conception until we were released of the astonishing breadth of that support.

Tom would remind us that our doleful experience was not unique. If we suffered from lack of food or from cold through scarce electricity and kerosene we were sharing the daily privations of many Iraqis and many millions more in the 'developing' world. Even our lack of freedom from mind-dulling routine was an experience in common with much of the world's population.

Every evening, following the CPT pattern, we had a time known as 'check in' when each of us was expected to tell the others how we had felt that day and whether there were any personal problems or difficulties between us. Jim and Tom were accustomed to this discipline and detailed their moods and their physical health. For Tom, his state depended much on the amount of sleep that he had had and on the quantity of food. Jim's mood was probably influenced by thwarted plans for escape, and on the quantity of food. It was during his bout of fever that Jim became very depressed.

Harmeet and I were not accustomed to sharing our inner thoughts in this way, possibly due to cultural differences, and generally said little in comparison to the other two. When I was in real despair and even started to contemplate suicide I did not share these thoughts.

I was 74 and had led a great life – was it worth sustaining under these conditions? My death might help the situation of the two remaining Canadians but there remained the problem of how to do it. If I took a large dose of beta-blockers would that stop my heart or merely reduce me to a cabbage? A mirror that could have been broken to make sharp shards was taken away at that time. A head-long dive from the upper landing onto the concrete stair below would probably result in a non-lethal injury. Then during one time of prayer I found myself saying 'When I get back to Pinner … '. Had I said those words? Yes, I had, and it meant that there was still hope and resilience within me. In the Old Testament (Exodus 3:14) God is called 'I am who I am' or 'I will be who I will be' – why not 'When I get back to Pinner'? So that became my new name for God. From that time on I took hope and decided to live out my life in captivity if necessary. I did share these thoughts about God at check in but not the suicidal ones. An additional rather mercenary thought was that every day I remained alive was worth about £20 to Pat, because our pension is reduced by 50 per cent on my death.

Some of the check-ins became rather repetitive and Tom would regularly complain about being a mere commodity to be bought or sold. After the umpteenth time I did object to this repetition. It was during check-in time that Tom revealed that on capture he had had his US military card with him from his days in the US Marine Band. He explained that it had been useful when taking Palestinians from Baghdad to the Syrian border. That military card was probably the explanation for much of the our captors' hostility towards Tom.

As the weeks passed we discovered a great deal about one another and it was one way of passing the time.

Tom Fox related that he was brought up in Chattanooga, Tennessee, where he went to school. His was a dysfunctional family with a mother who had a drink problem. However, he studied music at college and went on to become a clarinettist with the United States Marine Band. He lived in Washington, was married and had two children. Being part of the Marine Band involved a great deal of travelling and thus put a strain on his family relationships – this was one of the reasons why his wife and he were separated. After twenty years in the band Tom sought a new way of life and took a job with a chain of health food stores in the Virginia area south of Washington. In the 1980s Tom started attending a Quaker meeting for worship and later became a full member. He was active at his local meeting but also spent vacations helping at youth camps. After ten or twelve years working in the food stores he decided to make a further change in his life and applied to join the Christian Peacemaker Teams as a full-time member. He took the three-month CPT training course in Chicago in 2004 and started service in Palestine before moving on to Iraq. In Baghdad he helped in the collection of information about abuse in detention centres and took part in the evacuation of a group of Palestinians to the Syrian border. He also investigated the aftermath of the Coalition raid on Fallujah and helped in the subsequent clean-up. He talked to us about his daughter Katherine and son Andrew and proudly described their achievements.

Jim had had a different sort of upbringing in Canada, as part of a loving family at Saulte Ste Marie in Ontario. His education came under the care of the Basilian Brothers (followers of the fourth-century St Basil of Caesarea) and under their influence Jim decided to become a priest. After university he discerned that he was not suited to the priesthood and left the Basilians but sought other ways to serve within the Roman Catholic Church. He became very interested in the Catholic Worker movement, founded by the American peace activist Dorothy Day, and in 1990 founded Zacchaeus House in Toronto as a Catholic Worker house of hospitality, where he lived and worked for ten years with people who were homeless. Ten years on, Jim and others attempted to start a rural Catholic Worker community but without success, and he told us about the problems of looking after animals, birds and crops with the help of dysfunctional adults. In 2003 Jim had gone to Iraq with CPT before the invasion as leader of a large delegation, and had then worked as part of the team in Baghdad for three months. In 2004 he had become a programme co-ordinator in Canada and had been involved in overseeing a project in Kenora, Ontario in support of local efforts to stop racist treatment of the First Nations people who live there.

It was Jim who frequently expressed his frustration at missing out on the experiences of life. At the time I did not worry about how those months passed with such minimal sensory input. There was very little to stimulate the vision, touch, taste or feel, just a repetitive use of hearing. I came to appreciate Jim's point of view after our release when I had more sensual input in one hour's walk along the cliffs of Portland in Dorset than in all that time in captivity: sights of wild flowers, butterflies, the sea below, birds; sounds of the sea, a skylark overhead; smells from the sea and the foliage; the feel of the rocky path under my feet.

Harmeet's story was very different from the others. His family is Kashmiri and he had been born in Zambia where his father was a mining engineer. He began his education in Zambia and his family then sent him to England, starting at a preparatory school in Cirencester and then to St Edward's School in Oxford. He went on to Montreal where he studied computer engineering at McGill University. He had started playing squash while at school but honed his skill at university.

He talked to us a great deal about squash and the various opponents he had met in combat on the courts. He also liked to recount the plots of films he had seen but they invariably seemed to be violent ones. I objected, since my movie going has been largely limited to Wallace and Gromit sagas. I have wimpish sympathy with the lady who wanted an over-60s film certificate paralleling those for children.

When Harmeet left McGill he had worked in telecommunications firms and when his sister moved to New Zealand Harmeet decided to follow her. In New Zealand he was employed by a defence contractor designing simulation equipment for training soldiers. He became disillusioned with using his skills to support the war industry so he resigned and made a foray into active peace work with the International Solidarity Movement in Palestine. Back in New Zealand, he had decided he would move into a teaching career and take a degree in English Literature in preparation. He was worried about his possessions, which had been stored at his student flat in Auckland but only for a limited period.

It was at the end of the first year of studies that Harmeet applied to join the delegation to Iraq. He told us that although he came from a Sikh background he remains a seeker, although his grandparents were disappointed that he did not adopt the full Sikh identity. But they were proud of him for trying to live by Sikh principles.

Harmeet had met much racial prejudice and we discussed its roots and were given a long discourse by Jim on the topic. Jim had a tendency to hold forth at some length and used, in my opinion, unnecessary jargon such as 'pedagogy' when 'teaching' is a perfectly good English word. I did complain.

Other topics I remember discussing were anti-semitism (debating whether it had biblical roots in the New Testament), economic injustice and consumerism. (Jim had taken a particular dislike to Ikea, the Swedish chain of furniture stores.)

I contributed my autobiography, recounting various incidents in my past. On some occasions I talked about my two daughters and the life histories of my father's ten siblings (my six uncles and four aunts).

We also discussed the risks associated with the depleted uranium used in shell casings. This was a controversial subject, since I am of the opinion that the major dangers are chemical and not due to the very low level of radioactivity. I had a large disc of depleted uranium in my office in London at St Bartholomew's Hospital which had been used to define X-ray beams. I was aware that the dangers of radiation are often overstated by nuclear disarmers. I talked about areas of the world such as Brazil and India where people have lived for generations with very high natural levels of background radiation. The others were spared, by our release, a lecture on the theory of bone growth that I had started to prepare for them!

We recounted the life stories of some of our heroes. Tom talked about John Woolman, the American Quaker, Jim outlined the life and the achievements of Dorothy Day in starting the Catholic Worker movement and Harmeet talked about the founding gurus of the Sikh faith. I enlarged on the early history of the Baptist denomination and some of its heroes, such as William Carey, the pioneer missionary who appreciated the nobler aspects of the Hindu religion.

I used the wakeful hours in the night to recall details of the novels of Charles Dickens and was able to retell the stories of *David Copperfield, Nicholas Nickleby* and *Oliver Twist*. Jim also contributed stories from his Catholic Worker days and recalled some of his exciting canoeing exploits on the rapids of the remoter rivers of Canada. I talked (lectured?) about the subtleties of medical X-ray technology and told the saga of my strange hobby – taking photographs of baths in the countryside. A bath reused as a cattle trough or, in a garden, as a plant holder or pond, must be applauded as a 'green' recycled object. I have photographs of baths from all over Europe plus some from North America (see p. 131).

In addition there were many discussions about our situation. Each piece of news from Medicine Man would be dissected and analysed. We had soon realised that 'news' from Medicine Man was a series of lies and I opted out of the resulting conversations, asking that speculation take place in the morning since doleful thoughts would disturb my sleep.

Tom was probably the least talkative among us, although he had a rather penetrating voice that on occasions reverberated down the stairwell. The minders would then call up to us to be quiet! It was Tom who unexpectedly became a leader in speculation and would pronounce his theories for our future based on his knowledge of other kidnaps. He felt that his varied experiences gave him insights into the Iraqi way of thinking. I decided that we had to live as best we could day by day, not trying to guess what might occur. Jim would pronounce on how many days we had been in captivity. This I did not find helpful. Day 99 was just the same as day 100 and day 101 would probably have the same pattern.

Tom had a detailed knowledge of the fates of other detainees and had also done research with the CPT team on the torture of those detained by the Iraqi government. When Harmeet wanted to know more about the methods of torture I suggested that he talked to Tom quietly out of my earshot.

Tom and Jim spent many hours discussing their experiences of CPT training schemes and work. They analysed CPT policies and projects. Harmeet and I did not take part in these discussions, which occurred when Jim was seated next to Tom. But Jim did tell us all about earlier trips to Iraq. He had been there as a CPT member and then as leader of a delegation. It was on the former occasion that two Iraqi men talked their way into the apartment and then produced guns and demanded cash. After prolonged discussion one of the CPT women went to the office and brought out some of the cash which satisfied the robbers sufficiently, and they left.

The earlier delegation made a trip to the south, as we had been due to do. On the return journey, and travelling at fair speed to avoid attacks, the car James Loney was travelling in hit the rough ground at the side of the road and spun out of control, somersaulting onto the scrubby desert by the road. It was found that one of the delegates was missing and a brief search revealed him lying some distance from the wrecked car. Apparently he had been thrown out of the rear window. There were long delays in getting the man to a hospital but he had already died from his injuries. It was Jim's gruesome task to arrange for the body to be taken to Baghdad and by plane to the United States for burial.

I went through a phase of rankling at any mention of CPT because I blamed the Baghdad team for lack of care in getting us into this situation. That mosque was too isolated. When you have too much time to think you have to blame somebody other than yourself for your predicament. Since my release I have made a positive re-assessment of the true value of the work CPT has done in Iraq.

Two major topics were release and escape. It was Jim who fretted most about escape. Could we get onto the roof and escape by rope made from knotted strips of curtain? Could we break through a window in another room on our floor? Could we overpower one of our captors at exercise time and thus make our way out? There were a number of other diffi-culties to overcome. We didn't know where the house was situated with reference to a place of safety such as a police station or hospital. Could we get through the outside gates? And where were the keys to open the main doors kept? At first they were left lying on one of the beds, but they disappeared from view when we moved to the second room in the evenings.

Tom and Harmeet were against using any degree of force against the captors. I, in my cowardice, did not want to try any manoeuvre that was not guaranteed 99 per cent success. We did not try to escape, although there may have been a few times when we suspected that we were alone in the house. For any attempt at escape, the handcuffs presented no problem as we had now learned how to release these using the nail we had found in the sole of the shoe. But without keys to the padlocks, the welded chains linking us together were a barrier to free movement.

Tom worried about the ethics of being ransomed, since the money would go on weapons for the Mujahideen. I said that I just wanted to get the hell out of Baghdad by the quickest means possible and was not worried if that meant military transport. Jim, Tom and Harmeet were keen to return to the CPT apartment for a debriefing and to collect their belongings.

After Tom had been taken from us I had a feeling that Jim and Harmeet might think about escaping and leaving me behind, because I would not be able to climb down from a window. I thought it would be better if we all went or none of us. Jim and Harmeet said that if they got away they would be able to tell Pat and my family about my condition and where I was – or perhaps was not – by then.

In the days coming up to Christmas it became obvious that we were not to be released in time to join our families. This caused me great sadness and I recall at one check in asking permission to cry, which I did briefly to relieve the emotion. We did sing carols in the days coming up to Christmas and I tried to scratch a star into the plaster by my sleeping area. Jim wrote 'Christmas 2005' underneath the star.

In general I avoided thinking about Pat and about home. It was too painful. Although I did write this:

The Kidnap Widow

In deep mourning but not a widow yet,
trying to live a life – unable to forget.
Are conditions harsh? Is he in pain?
Such thoughts distress the sleepless brain.
Though friends assure, 'No news is good',
she silently weeps in her widowhood.

9

WHISTLER'S MOTHER AND OTHER DIVERSIONS

Life is much too important to be taken seriously.
Oscar Wilde

When I try to recollect the hundreds of hours spent together, it seems that there was very little laughter and few jokes. But we did keep a sense of humour in many of our interactions, for example in the games. I have an overdeveloped sense of the absurd that prevented me from taking part in some of the more earnest and serious discussions that seemed irrelevant to our status as captives.

Tom was very concerned about press coverage at the time of our release and we all rehearsed our response to press interrogation. My feeling was that I would worry about this when and if we were released – although I did write a few ideas for a press release in my notebook. These ideas foreshadowed much of what I said in my first press statement at Heathrow.

We managed to get by with relatively few rows. When you are handcuffed together most actions with the hands demand the co-operation of the others. Thus writing, eating, passing a beaker of water and adjusting clothes or scratching required co-operative movement from one or other of your neighbours. Although I generally did have a free left hand – we did change places from time to time – any action with the right hand needed the permission of Jim or Harmeet or Tom.

Arguments on some issues got heated, but tempers were generally kept in check because we had to live together in such close proximity. There were no periods of not talking to each other. I must have had habits and manners of speech which annoyed the others. Certainly, my snoring kept Jim awake as I had periods of apnoea when you seem, alarmingly, to stop breathing and then start up again with a snort. I also have a tendency to make odd sound-effects to accompany movements such as getting up in the morning.

For me it was the pronunciation of Toronto as 'Torono' or water as 'warder' that was my chief dislike. I suffered indigestion for most of the captivity, and there were frequent emissions of gas from both ends of my alimentary canal. I also fear that Jim thought me a bit careless over matters of hygiene, although I am sure that after a few weeks we must have shared all of each others' bacterial flora.

There was one occasion when Harmeet and I were recalling the poems of William Blake:

Tyger! Tyger! burning bright
in the forests of the night,
what immortal hand or eye
could frame thy fearful symmetry?

Jim objected to the poor rhyme and described it as 'snucky'. I was furious at this insult to a highly-regarded English poet and said that he could only criticise when he could write as well as Blake. This touched a sore point in Jim's consciousness and he rose in anger – how dare I tell him what he could or could not say? Later we sought reconciliation and achieved a working level of forgiveness.

I had taken the initiative in asking for things in the early days because it was thought that the kidnappers would show respect for my age. Later on Jim took the initiative in nearly all requests to improve our condition. He suggested early on that we be given notebooks to relieve our boredom. After repeated requests, four notebooks similar to school copy-books were eventually provided, with a biro for each of us. This was at the beginning of February. Later we asked for books in English – a Bible or Qur'an – but although these were promised, they never arrived. Harmeet also requested an English dictionary to help with preparation for his degree course. Large print editions would be needed if I were to read them without glasses.

When the notebooks arrived Jim spent a great deal of time trying to remember what had happened to us since our capture so that he could compile a detailed diary. He wanted to record the exact wording of our conversations with the captors in his notebook. He had in mind writing a play about our experience – a sort of Baghdad Endgame. He sought the necessary information by questioning the rest of us, although I resigned from talking about early harrowing events. Jim's absorbing project meant that we did not necessarily keep to our schedule of worship and study, and Tom felt that an important spiritual resource to keep us mentally healthy was being lost. He also asked for a 30-minute period of silence each day because Jim, Harmeet and I chatted away for long periods on various secular topics His request was granted.

Harmeet kept an outline diary of events – the visits of Medicine Man, videos, unusual meals, clothes-washing days and so on. Tom wrote rather little but set out his thoughts in the form of mental maps, diagrams which the captors found rather suspicious. From time to time they would leaf through our notebooks. Harmeet wrote long lists of the things he had to do when he was released, but sadly this list had to be revised from time to time as deadlines for action were passed.

His next pre-occupation was to turn the patterns he saw in the torn wallpaper into creatures, faces and objects, although he never visualised the upside-down submarine that I could see. Harmeet is skilful as an artist and he made a sketch of a rose that was brought to us and gave the sketch to me as a present for my wife (see p. 205). Near the end of our period of captivity he started a new collection of drawings, this time of the captors' mobile phones.

When Harmeet was sitting by Tom, food was often the topic. Harmeet sought advice on cooking utensils and on vegetarian menus he could cook for himself as a solitary student. Tom provided a range of ideas based on Quorn and these were carefully recorded in Harmeet's notebook.

Before the notebooks arrived our diversions needed to be verbal. Word play such as transforming words one letter at a time e.g. 'black' to 'white' (black, slack, slick, slice, spice, spine, shine, whine, white) or 'fast' to 'slow' (fast, past, post, host, hoot, soot, slot, slow) can be performed in the mind. We also tried some mathematical exercises with prime numbers and discovered that 2006 can be analysed as $2 \times 17 \times 59$.

There were a number of other diversions that we used to pass the time. We went through the alphabet thinking of fruits and then animals with names that started with each letter. Then we spent much time just listening – listening attentively to sounds from downstairs and listening to sounds from outside the house.

There was a curfew each night from 10.00 pm until morning so that the only traffic sounds at night were military vehicles. There were fewer commercial sounds on Friday mornings – the Islamic holy day – and there were silent days before and during the election on 15 December for a permanent National Assembly. We had seen the posters for this election when we arrived in Baghdad. Afterwards we asked Medicine Man about the election but he was fairly cynical and took the point of view of many Iraqis. The election was an American fix. He did not think it was a truly democratic process. Following major events like the bombing by insurgents of the 1,200-year-old Shia Golden Mosque in Samara on 22 February, there were days of curfew to prevent inter-community clashes.

Early one Friday morning there was the sound of many trucks arriving and departing and a great banging of propane cylinders. Tom thought this was illegal selling of propane – there are black markets for many goods in Baghdad. Nephew was heard to rush out with a cylinder to be filled or exchanged. All these commonplace sounds from the outside world emphasised our own isolation.

I recorded an Alphabet of Sounds (explanatory notes which I have added to the original are in italics):

A   Aircraft to freedom
B   Birds (*Small birds, with some that made a 'pswit, pswit' sound in the mornings*)
     Buses (*a guess based on noises of stopping vehicles accompanied by voices*)
C   Cats (*there was a kitten that came into the downstairs room from time to time and Uncle would feed it*)
D   Dogs (*a chain reaction of barking, building up to a great crescendo at night*)
E   Explosions (*generally two or three a day. Tom would always pray immediately for the victims*)
F   Football crowds (*when guns would be fired into the air – the loudest and longest burst of gunfire occurred when Iraq beat Syria*)
     Fireworks (*at the festival of Eid*)
G   Gunfire
     Generators
     Gate to driveway (*closing with a bang*)

H   Helicopters
     Horns and hooters
I
J   Jets
K
L   Loudspeakers (*making election announcements and other
     public information items*)
M   Marriages (*gunfire again*)
N   Night Patrols (*there was always a convoy of military trucks
     just before the call to prayer*)
O   Owls
     Outside door banging
P   Prayer calls (*these were most obvious at about 5.00 am but
     they continued at intervals throughout the day, and seemed to
     be much longer at the Eid-al-Adha festival in January*)
     Propane gas sellers (*often using donkey carts as transport but
     advertising their wares by banging on the cylinders*)
Q
S   Sirens associated with police or ambulances
T   Thunder (*we experienced two or three thunderstorms*)
V   Voices (*some were from outside the house and some from
     within. Junior always spoke in a strident voice and could be
     easily distinguished*)
     Visitors (*these were rare*)
W   Winds blew the curtains, and in storms brought in a
     thin film of sand on all surfaces

Even when the notebooks arrived we still needed diversions
when the electricity failed and we were unable to see. We
continued with details of our life stories and tried puzzles
based on guessing historical figures ('Whistler's Mother' took
a long time to track down with questions answered by 'yes' or
'no'). Another device was the telling of three stories from our
experience – for example, I claimed to have broken my nose

on three occasions, once on an icy slide, once when hit by a golf club and once by walking into a plate glass door. The others had to decide which stories were true and which were false (in this case, the last one was false).

Eventually we were given a pair of socks each. These came with a piece of card attached. I saw that these cards could be used for games. They were blue on one side and plain on the other. I tore them up and thought initially that we could use them for noughts and crosses (Tic Tac Toe), but realised that with 24 pieces we could develop a better game. This was based on a 5 by 5 square with the centre position blocked by an empty medicine holder. The two players had 12 cards each, either blue side up or the reverse. We then took it in turns to place the cards so that we made horizontal, vertical or diagonal runs of three or more cards. We developed a number of variations on this game e.g. who could get the lowest score? Uncle saw us with the cards and showed us a simple Iraqi game which he called Jelgay, and henceforward that was the name we gave to our diversions.

It should be recorded that although we played games on most days, when the mood was bleak there was reluctance to play and our inertia had to be overcome if only to help pass the time. The games became a discipline – almost like prayer.

I took some time making pieces from a toothpaste box for a game of Draughts (Chequers) but it took so long to set out the 64 squares and 24 pieces that we only played it a few times. When the notebooks arrived I spent three mornings carefully tearing 52 identical pieces of paper. These I intended to use as a set of playing cards, but knowing that Muslims object to gambling, I marked them as A (1–13), B(1–13) and so on. The cards were about 4 by 3 cm and I had problems in reading them without glasses. We did try playing games as a foursome, but it was not easy when seated side by side. I'm afraid that I used the cards by myself for daily games of patience (I know six or seven different games). I taught Harmeet one of the more interesting games of patience (called Calculation or Broken Intervals) which requires plenty of thought, but not much space. Eventually the pieces of paper became so greasy that many of the numbers on the cards could be read from the reverse side.

I was aggrieved that I could not think up a use for the round cheese boxes, although the minders did use one of them for a candle holder. One cheese container was like a match box with a drawer – it came with four square cheeses in it, and I used it as a holder for the playing cards and the Jelgay cards.

The notebooks were used for a series of competitive games: for example, how many words could be made out of the letters making up 'reconciliation'? Following the 'Wheel of Fortune' pattern we tried to guess a common phrase, a letter at a time, from the pattern of letters ('Good morning' would be - - - -   - - - - - - -). Jim made some cards that we

The cheese box, with our homemade playing cards and Jelgay cards (Ian Britton, *Baptist Times*)

picked at random from a plastic bag to mimic the values assigned in dollars to each correct guess and also the hazards on the wheel of fortune used in the TV show. I saw little point in putting monetary values ($100 to $1,000) on the guesses we made, and would cheat by offering up low frequency letters like Q or Z so that I always lost.

Jim had a tendency to make encouraging remarks during games: 'That's a good word', 'That was a good move.' I had the impression that he liked to be in control. On the whole we kept such sources of annoyance to ourselves and out of courtesy did not complain.

My technique for dealing with our situation was to shut my mind down into a dozing state. I generally did not talk until after midday. I preferred to occupy my mind by recalling past events, times at work or on holiday. I drew a rough map of France in my notebook because we had had so many good holidays in France, either camping with the girls or with just Pat and myself in cottages and rural hotels. In addition to the map of France, I sketched some English cathedrals and outlined details of church architecture. I took a mental trip round the coast of Britain, trying to recall each seaside town or port. I shared my recollection of a favourite view – a rabbit-frequented hill overlooking the sweep of Weymouth Bay with the Isle of Portland in the background.

Tom walked us along his best-remembered trail through his beloved Appalachian Mountains. We talked about favourite art galleries and museums and I am sure that I shared my enthusiasm for the plaster galleries in the Victoria and Albert Museum in London with full-scale reproductions of famous sculptures and architectural features (Michelangelo's statue of David has a detachable fig leaf that was put in position when Queen Victoria was on a visit). Other geographic mental exercises on my part were counting British cathedrals and football clubs. My memory gave totals

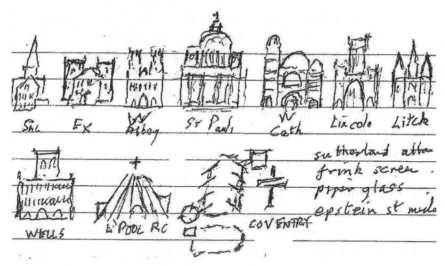

My sketches of English cathedrals

of 40 cathedrals and 44 soccer clubs. I also drew a plan of my garden in Pinner and marked the positions of the major plants – and of the weeds.

So I used my notebook for a range of purposes, although without glasses I could only read and write when the light was bright. I use that as an excuse for my poor handwriting and spelling in the notebook. In the first pages I wrote a few words in Arabic – the numbers from 1 to 10 and then essential words like *shukran* (thank you), *zaine* and *muzaine* (good and bad) and *mushkalar* (problem). I also noted the words for soldier (*jaish*), church (*kinese*) and today (*neom*). Both Jim and Harmeet built more extensive lexicons of Arabic.

In trying to remember geometrical theorems I drew the constructions necessary for the proof of Pythagoras' theorem and for the alternate segment theorem. I also attempted to reconstruct log tables to base 10 and algebraic formulae such as that for solving quadratic equations (Harmeet recalled the derivation of that).

When I asked Medicine Man for reading glasses (they were always coming the 'next week') I managed to write out the formulae for lenses in the terms used by opticians – i.e. focal lengths in dioptres. I even tried, unsuccessfully, to construct my own Sudoku puzzles.

And I wrote doggerel – some of it only partially in rhyme:

> Our God, our God, why have you forsaken us,
> just when the mujahideen had taken us?
> Do you watch our cycles of despair
> as hopes of freedom vanish in thin air?
> Or do you work more subtly,
> reminding us from time to time of the places, faces,
> little details of home –
> the fact that although ten thousand deaths occur
>   around us,
> and each is significant,
> our lives have value because we are loved.

Although there was plenty of time for meditation I had problems improving my ability to meditate. I always get distracted too easily. The technique of using the imagination to live within a New Testament story has always evaded me but I did manage to picture my way through the story of Jesus arriving at a village where the children came to meet him, although the disciples tried to rebuke them for worrying him. Perhaps my visit to Israel in 1994 helped me to visualise the scene. I did write out my own prayer scheme for the week with a daily biblical thought and subjects for intercession.

I also wrote out a list of parables and remembered people in my church by an alphabetical list of members' names which I was able to transfer to paper when the notebook arrived. I worked hard during the nights to recall the words of hymns but generally managed only one or two verses. They were favourites like 'Worship the Lord in the Beauty of Holiness' and 'My Song Is Love Unknown'. This latter hymn seemed to speak to our condition as it details the rejection and death of Jesus.

I wrote the remembered verses in my notebook – the list includes about 21 hymns – and when these verses were copied out in large capitals I would use them for worship sessions. For hymns unknown to the others I had to use a croaky solo voice although Harmeet had encountered some of the hymns during his days at schools in England. I recall that he asked for William Blake's 'And Did Those Feet in Ancient Times', and so we sang together that anthem of the Women's Institute.

In addition to hymns, I rehearsed in my mind the Major General's song from *The Pirates of Penzance*. I had taken that role in a school production but I hope that I did not inflict a rendition of it upon my fellows.

Harmeet took my notebook to write a few directions on contacting his relatives for me to follow if I survived and he did not. I thought about a possible ransom and did a rough calculation of the money that could be available to my wife if the house was re-mortgaged. It was well under the two million that Medicine Man told us they were seeking as a ransom for each of us. And then there was the fact that CPT are against all ransom deals. On one occasion we were asked to make pleas to Sheikh Hamad, the Prince of Qatar and to Sheikh Khalifa bin Zayed Al Nahyan, ruler of Abu Dhabi and President of the United Arab Emirates. (We learned afterwards that certain sheikhs did offer at one stage to provide a ransom for us.) I composed a note for Pat that elliptically referred to money-raising ideas. It was fortunately never used, and Pat received no request for a ransom. If I had thought it would help I would have given the note to Medicine Man to be transmitted to Pat in some way.

I wrote brief letters to Pat, my daughters and grandson, and to Bob Gardiner my minister, so that they might read them if I were killed and my notebook survived.

From Pat I asked her forgiveness for causing her so much anguish and said 'thank you for taking the risk of marrying me 44 years ago'. I thanked the family and my minister for looking after Pat under these stressful conditions. In the letter to my grandson, to be read when he was 18 or so, I explained my reasons for going to Iraq.

To be read when Ben comes to maturity:

> From captivity:
> You will know by now that I came to believe that violence was not the answer to conflict situations. Violence tends to lead to further violence – maybe at a much later date. So better ways have to be found to resolve disputes between people, communities and nations. So your grandfather was active in many peace movements. Feeling that writing letters to MPs and going on demonstrations was 'easy peacemaking', he decided to explore the Christian Peacemaker approach which involves taking risks in conflict zones. In Grandad's case it brought him many weeks of captivity as a kidnap victim with three others.
>
> I would not wish you to share that experience but hope that you will take account of values of truth, justice and peace in the path you choose to follow through life – and marry someone who combines the best qualities of your mum and grandma!
> Norman

I wished to keep my mind occupied for future months and made a list in my notebook of projects that I would complete in due time. I roughed out but did not manage to complete large-scale diagrams for a lecture on bone growth, my field of expertise. The problems of projecting a world map, a globe, onto a cube became evident when the project was started. I try to excuse my poor draughtsmanship by my lack of reading glasses and the inability to erase mistakes.

Designs for a set of Stations of the Cross based on our experiences were never completed but I drew a small outline of a painting by Georges Rouault. It depicts Jesus during his trials passing under an archway with a grinning gargoyle above. It spoke to me in our condition. Then I started on a Captives' Cyclopaedia, beginning with Aardvark, Anatomy and Architecture. Each article was to have two sections, one being memorised facts and the second current observation. (Harmeet knew that aardvaaks live in Zambia!)

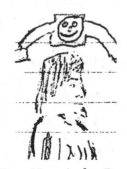

'Ecce Homo' after Rouault

Architecture: *Experienced* All square block on three floors including roof. About 12 rooms, very secure with high walls and metal grilles and gates. Stone floors – hot weather.

Remembered Developed in all world from lintels to arches depending on building materials. Columns

[116]

became complex as surfaces are decorated. 'Modern' designs rely on concrete, plastics and glass.

Anatomy: *Experienced* The bits of bone that stick out and make sitting or lying for 12 hours painful e.g. hip bones, ribs, coccyx, as muscle and fat waste away.

Harmeet also submitted an article:

Film: *Remembered* An escape from the mores of daily life with an occasional flourish of insight.
Experienced An escape from the thought of escape.

I finish this chapter with my drawing of a snakes and ladders board that summarises the last two chapters. Each ladder was labelled A to K and the snakes L to U.

Ladders

A   Wash down self and some clothes
B   Fragrant rose brought in from garden
C   Shave with ancient electric razor
D   Christmas cake brought in by Nephew
E   Two good meals in one day
F   Kill mosquitoes
G   Four toothbrushes arrive
H   Go downstairs to watch *Zorro*
I   Electric fire fixed up
J   Bag of dates provided before bed
K   Notebooks arrive

Snakes

L   No *carbara* (electricity)
M   Woken at 8.00 am – a long day ahead
N   Just three chips in bread
O   Sensodyne toothpaste finally used up

P   Night emergency – grenades
Q   Uncle says, 'No money, no release'
R   Yet another video made
S   Uncle tries to convert us to Islam
T   (The longest snake) Medicine man says, 'Release in one day/two days'
U   Use *hammam* bottle

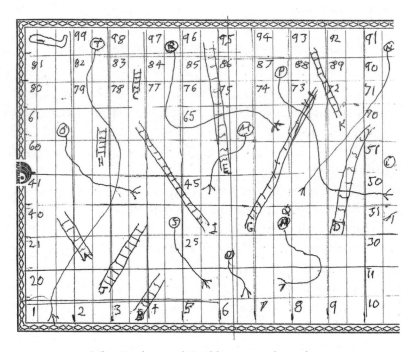

The Snakes and Ladders – see key above

10

THE DAILY CAPTIVE

Would that we could follow the birds!
Norman Kember

The monotony of our daily life induced a false sense of security. If nothing good was happening to us then nothing bad was going to happen either. Banner headlines on *The Daily Captive* might change from 'Jim achieves 20 press-ups today' to 'Harmeet beats Norman at Jelgay by six points'. The rest of the paper would show no difference in content from one day to the next. But about once a week something out of the ordinary routine occurred and, provided that it was not too threatening, it at least alleviated the boredom.

In December and January we would hear a voice from outside the house It sounded like '*Aled*' to me but Jim and Harmeet disagreed: they said it was '*Ahmed*'. I thought '*Aled*' was some sort of 'hello' greeting from a visiting neighbour. It certainly preceded the arrival of somebody. Junior or Nephew would welcome this visitor and we were told to keep quiet for the duration of their stay. Whoever the neighbour was, he must have sensed a certain hesitation in his welcome and eventually gave up the visits.

Once we heard sounds downstairs of a small group of visitors arriving. The voices included that of a woman and to our surprise the visitors seemed to be looking over the house.

The Daily Mail, 30 November 2005

Uncle slid into the room with us, took the chains off the door and held it shut. To our amazement the visitors started coming upstairs. The group appeared to inspect all the rooms on our floor and even tried to enter ours but Uncle's firm grip on the handle prevented them. I wonder if lives would have been at risk had we called out – but what is the Arabic

for 'Help – we are kidnap victims'? We were given to understand that our captors had rented this house and these were
potential buyers or renters for the future.

One night there was the sound of an armoured convoy
stopping near to the house – heavy trucks and tracked
vehicles. Evidently a troop of soldiers were conducting house
raids in the area, looking for weapons and suspected insurgents. Uncle and Junior came bursting into our room saying
that we were about to be attacked. They had grenades in their
hands and were obviously prepared to use them. They cannot
have had a strategy for repulsing such an attack or they would
have gone into one of the other rooms that overlooked either
the road or the driveway to the house.

Our room, with its pile of furniture by the window, was
not at all a suitable place from which to launch a counter-
attack. The armed convoy moved off and the 'emergency' was
over. There was no repeat, although Uncle claimed to have
spent one night sitting at a side window with a rocket
launcher because he feared that an attack was likely through
the side gate! The possibility of such a raid made Jim feel that
we were continually in danger, since the captors could have
had orders to kill us in such an eventuality.

As I mentioned earlier, we had discovered how to release
the handcuffs. I recall that I was the first to do this with the
nail that we found in the sole of the shoe, but Harmeet
became the expert. Our kidnappers had found curtains for us
to use as floor cover and these were well supplied with
curtain hooks which could be made into alternatives to the
nail – the instrument of grace! We used this facility at night
and it enabled me to roll over and sleep on my left side. Once
or twice I used my freedom to stand up to ease my pelvic
pains but was nearly caught by a surprise night time visit from
Uncle and so I gave up standing in this way.

We always took care to click our handcuffs on again in the

early morning and the minders did not discover this skill of ours, although there were some close calls.

Jim worried greatly over the captor-captive relationship and felt that we were too compliant in order to make life easy for ourselves. The handcuffs were often offered to us to put on ourselves. We refused, saying that the task of shackling us was theirs.

After Tom had been taken, Jim and Harmeet took turns to be chained to the door but then it was decided that we should no longer release the handcuffs at night because in the warmer weather we did not sleep under the protective cover of the thick opaque blanket. I therefore asked to sleep with my wrist chained to the door because I could then sleep on my left side. My right side was still very sore from the early days. It was at this stage that a great deal of slack in the chain was given to me so that I could reach the *hammam* during the night, although I was cautioned not to make too much noise! The chains were heavy and strong with welded links and it required some skill to make the crossing without any noise. As the weather grew warmer we were provided with the two patterned sheets and set of pillow cases (made in India). The sheet covered the, by now, dirty futon and the cases covered the equally dirty pillows.

During the day we would occasionally go on 'expeditions'. Although connected together we were able to move across the room in a line (like chorus girls), revolving about the person chained to the door. This movement was used to fetch items like medicines from their place on the hostess trolley, to fix the electric heater or put rubbish in the bin. One day on such a trip I moved the curtain to look at the disused bird's nest that lay between the window and the bars. At this moment Nephew walked in and said that he would have to report this misconduct. We were always afraid of being further confined in extra shackles. Jim mimed that I was a bird watcher and Nephew said that he would not report it this time. Subsequently I wrote:

We are not allowed to lift the corner of the curtain
to look at the old bird's nest
that lies between the glass and the bars.
Would that we could follow the birds!

Medicine Man's visits once every ten days or a fortnight were anticipated with mixed feelings: pleasure, because we hoped to hear good news; and dislike, because we had soon learned that nearly all he said was lies. We always tried to engage him in conversation and initially we invariably asked for information about our release. Later on, we agreed in advance the other requests that we were going to make – food, wash-downs or medicines – and who would be the spokesperson. Medicine Man generally started by enquiring about our health and went on to explain the latest phase in negotiations for our release. Jim's notes record the reasons we were given for imminent release and the excuses we received as to why it failed to occur. In the first category, Jim lists 'prisoner exchanges' and 'ransoms from various Muslim leaders from Jordan to the Gulf States'. 'Only a phone call and you will be free', dissimulated Medicine Man.

The excuses included CIA interference, problems in moving currency across borders, delays in flights by couriers and problems in moving us to a safe house in the city due to checkpoints. Another excuse was re-organisation of their group following the capture of one of the leaders. This capture might have been more significant than we realised if it were evidence that the intelligence services were on the trail of our kidnappers. Medicine Man was a skilled liar. He often told us that we were world famous and I replied that it was not a fame that I had in any way desired.

On one occasion he stopped in front of Tom and told him that he, Medicine Man, had had experience in intelligence work and therefore knew exactly what sort of devious man Tom was. He stood face to face with Tom and told him menacingly that in the event of any trouble Medicine Man would have him killed. We all objected to this, saying that Tom was a man of peace and that Medicine Man did not understand him, not having met a man like Tom before.

Interactions with the minders generally occurred at meal times or at night. They usually ignored me and tried to talk to Jim or Harmeet. Occasionally during the day when they were particularly bored, one of them would come up and try to engage us in conversation. With Uncle we talked about gardens – I drew a plan of mine – and once he sat on the small metal seat in front of us and gave us a long lecture on Islam. He informed us that Islam was superior because of its belief in the one God while Christianity was obviously at fault because we allowed cremation! Much of this 'lecture' was in mime.

With Nephew we discussed families and with Junior the state of his love-life and the health of his sister. The minders were surprised that my wife was only two years younger than I, as a difference of ten years was evidently the norm in Iraq. It was Nephew who came in with reports of having seen my wife (Madame) and my grandson on the television. I could only guess how this was possible, being unaware that Pat had made several appeals on television with Al Jazeera camera crews coming to the house. Jim spent a great deal of time trying with words and mime to persuade Junior that his life was too valuable for him to become a suicide bomber.

At about the end of January there was a break in our routine. On some evenings we were released, put on our shoes, picked up the drinking beakers and were led down-stairs into the minders' room. This was the room in which

Tom and I had been originally introduced to the house. I think the minders were trying to make sure we did not get too depressed and Medicine Man would have given the necessary permission for this jaunt downstairs.

Two minders were always on duty in the evening. There were two beds in the downstairs room, one of which was used by Junior or Nephew for sleeping and the other as a general receptacle for food, keys, towels, clothes and rubbish. Uncle had his bed made up on the floor.

There was a fan in the ceiling and a pair of remarkably fancy lights with petal-shaped glass shades and hanging bunches of glass balls. A coat stand stood against one wall and the full length curtains were always pulled. There was a small low table with a mosaic top and curved legs which was used to hold sundry bottles of drink and cups.

I was generally found a chair and the others sat on the floor. Food was often provided, as I mentioned earlier. We then watched the TV. If the power failed a generator kicked in and the TV set powered up again. The alternatives on offer were TV newscasts, sports programmes or Iraqi soap operas.

We were also shown DVDs of the Mujahideen at work blowing up American armoured vehicles, sniping at soldiers or releasing mortar bombs. If a Coalition soldier was killed in an incident, the minders would re-run it and exclaim 'Rejoice!' We objected and said that the death of any person, American or Iraqi, was a tragedy. Then there were the DVDs of films. We watched a Zorro film at least twice (as innocent as a Lone Ranger episode – a masked ranger who galloped about righting wrongs). Then there were violent films like *Timecop*, *Mr and Mrs Smith*, *Transporter II* or *Banlieu 13*. The DVD player was long-suffering. If the disc drawer failed to come out it was prised open with a knife or the whole player given a hefty thump by Uncle.

We were shown the same films several times. I did not

watch the violent ones on their repeat showing and therefore I looked for diversions. I counted 20 glass balls in the hanging bunch on the light fitting before us, but Harmeet made it 21.

Jim and Harmeet would take their notebooks downstairs with them to work on their writing or sketching projects. When the biros were running dry the minders produced an old container with a variety of wax crayons and a number of pens, but they were all dried out. On some evenings we watched a programme called *Just for Laughs – GAGS*, a Canadian half-hour of practical jokes without commentary. Jim found these very funny and laughed aloud. I considered some of the incidents amusing but have never thought practical jokes to be pain-free.

Medicine Man came one day with a two-disc film about the life of Jesus. It had been provided by a friend of his daughter and had been made by a Christian group in Iraq. It was a simple but well-made film with commentary and dialogue in Arabic but we could follow the general trend of the material presented. It started with Adam, Abraham and Isaac before embarking on John the Baptist and then the Christmas story. In describing the mission of Jesus there was an emphasis on healing miracles but the parable of the Good Samaritan was told as an inset drama. The events of Holy Week included a re-enactment of the last supper, which was taken in good Eastern style with the disciples seated in a circle on the ground and dipping their portions of the flat bread into the dish (this resonated with our practice in captivity).

The rest of the Easter story was told in admirable detail and after the resurrection there was a recap when, I guess, the Gospel message was underlined. I don't know what our captors made of this film. Bizarrely, it was followed by sport on the television – Manchester United versus Everton.

At the beginning of March the downstairs venue was

changed to the room immediately below ours (see the plan of the house on page 72). The reason for this change was not clear. The space the minders now put to use was part of a much larger room that ran the length of the house. There was a modern room divider with cupboards, shelves and glass-fronted cabinets in dark wood, much as you might buy at a good Western furniture store. The shelves of the divider were thick with dust and held a few bowls, some large books, an electronic box (possibly a tape recorder), the prayer mat and a copy of the Qur'an with a reading stand.

The farther part of the room appeared to be furnished with traditional chairs and sofas but the section in use had the television set and a floor lamp that was only partly freed from its delivery wrappings. They had brought the small table from the first room and the three plastic chairs against the wall on which we sat.

One wall of this room lay alongside the driveway into the house. The large window was in this wall and it was always curtained off. There were no beds in this room so both minders presumably slept on the carpet. Uncle, as always, kept a revolver under his pillow and, by Harmeet's account, spent some time cleaning his weapons, including an AK-47 type rifle. But this weapon was never on display in the evening.

A number of videos were taken of us, again using a small hand-held camera. After one visit from Video Man, who had filmed us at the first house, Medicine Man took over the duties of camera operator.

Having taken the first video, Medicine Man was unable to replay the sequence on the camera's small screen until Harmeet came to his rescue and showed him the correct buttons to press for rewind and view. I recall that after one video session when Uncle and Junior were present with Medicine Man, Uncle made some remark and they started to laugh at us. I objected and tried to say that while it was *harran* (unclean) to walk on carpets with shoes in Iraq, in our country it was *harran* to laugh at people in misfortune. Medicine Man excused them by saying that Uncle was well known as a joker.

11

A TRAGEDY CONCEALED

If I am ever called upon to make the ultimate sacrifice in love of enemy, I trust that God will give me the grace to do so.

Tom Fox

Tom Fox with Palestinian children

In mid-February it was presented to us that release was at hand ('*Inshallah*' – 'God willing') and that in order to facilitate a smooth hand-over to the authorities it would be necessary to move us back to the first house, which was nearer to the mosque from whence we would be set free.

We were told that the first to be moved would be Tom and myself. Junior came upstairs and excitedly repeated this pronouncement, pointing to Tom and me. Tom gathered his spare clothes and notebook and was given a plastic bag to put them in. Junior made a great fuss, kissing Tom and myself and Tom was led downstairs. I have forgotten how Tom took this separation but he certainly embraced Jim and Harmeet before leaving. I then gathered my possessions and bundled them up ready for the next transport – but it never came. When Uncle entered the room I indicated by pointing to the bundle of clothes: 'When is it my turn to be moved?' Uncle looked surprised, as if I was talking nonsense.

It was in this way that Tom was separated from us on 12 February. We regularly asked how Tom was faring and were told that he keeping well and was reading books. All the minders and Medicine Man kept repeating this. We thought and prayed a great deal about Tom and the ordeal of being in captivity by himself.

Finally Medicine Man told us that in order to put pressure on the British and Canadian governments a message was being put out that Tom had been killed. We were, however, to be assured that Tom was still alive. We half believed this story, but came to realise that it was more than likely that Tom had in fact been killed. The minders continued the myth that Tom was still alive. He would be reunited with us when we were all four released together. We did not discover the truth, that Tom had been shot and his body dumped by the roadside, until our release.

Shortly after Tom was taken away Medicine Man came

with the video camera and said the British had sent three questions for me to answer that would prove that I was alive. These were questions supplied by Pat. The first one demanded my full names and those of my wife. The second asked for the words engraved on my ring. This was an odd question because I have never had a ring. I suggested that the query might refer to the unique ring that Pat possessed – it had been specially adapted for her by a jeweller in the City of London. The final question asked about my 'strange hobby' and how I had started it. This related to my collection of photographs of baths in the countryside, which in turn resulted from stories about the adventures of a bath called Albert that I had told to my daughters.

To reinforce the answers to the questions that I spoke onto tape, I also wrote them down hurriedly on a piece of paper. Because the second question was strange, I did wonder if Medicine Man had been able to concoct the three questions himself by discovering from Tom the details of my collection

An example from my collection! Bath tub by the Sea of Galilee

of bath photographs. In spite of our mistrust, the questions were in fact genuine although the ring question was not what she had asked. The Foreign Office in London had asked Pat to compose them.

We did wonder how the questions had been sent to Medicine Man. We also wondered how the videotapes of ourselves were passed back to our governments – perhaps via Al Jazeera? The sheet of paper on which I wrote the answers to Pat's questions (or a copy) arrived safely in London. Four Foreign Office officials paid a visit to our home and presented the paper, without prior explanation, to Pat. She was able to confirm that the handwriting was mine, although it was very shaky.

The next two videos made by Medicine Man related to the 'Canadians First' story that was promulgated once again in March. Jim and Harmeet were videoed holding the day's newspaper so that the date was verifiable. The possibility of Jim and Harmeet being released made me feel depressed at the thought of being left as sole captive. However, I was con-soled by the fact that any person released would be able to inform Pat of our true situation. I worked out and rehearsed what I would like the Canadians to say to her if they were released.

The captors all liked Harmeet and trusted him to help with food preparation, the cleaning and the clothes washing. Harmeet did, then, get to see the kitchen with its large refrig-erator, a gas cooker, a sink and a table. He told us that the kitchen and the rest of the house were in general disarray and that although there was a vacuum cleaner under the stairs it was never used. The wearing of shoes on the carpet was strictly forbidden but the same carpet had a fair covering of oddments of food and even nail clippings.

The downstairs stone floors were cleaned from time to time. On occasion Harmeet was directed to do the cleaning and his job was to pour on water and apply a squeegee. But this merely redistributed the dirt, since there was no drain for the messy water.

One evening he was called downstairs to attach a video player to the TV but had a problem explaining that the minders did not have the correct leads to make the connection. I was somewhat envious of Harmeet, since such expeditions downstairs made a break in the boring routine of the day.

The captors had made it clear that they regarded me as a bit of a wimp and invariably tried to talk only to Jim and Harmeet. Jim complained that Uncle and Junior did not show me sufficient respect as an elderly man – seniors are traditionally treated with consideration in the Arab world.

The two Canadians made some effort to increase their Arabic vocabularies and Harmeet found that some Arab words were similar to Punjabi words he knew because of his Sikh background. I forgot new words from one day to the next.

There was a particular interaction with our minders when Jim massaged Junior's back. Junior had been complaining about his back and on inspection Jim told him that he had a range of knotted muscles which massage and pressure could relieve. Junior appreciated the massage, which took place either during exercise time or at night when Junior lay prone on one of the beds downstairs.

Cheap disposable razors appeared from time to time but these were useless without hot water and soap. On one foraging expedition Uncle came in with an ancient electric hair trimmer. This was persuaded to work by the usual procedure of inserting the bare wires into an electric socket. At first I allowed Uncle to trim my beard by the downstairs sink but later I did my own work with the device. A large mirror was brought into our room and the trimmer wires thrust into our electricity socket. The remains of my beard covered the floor and took some time to clear up. It was great to see my face with less of a covering of grey hairs – I looked more like me! In a later episode I allowed Junior to try his skills as a barber as my hair had grown well over the ears. From my view of the front Junior appeared to have done a fair job. But the back, Jim said, was a disaster – very uneven and in obviously stepped layers.

Jim and Harmeet trimmed their beards with a small pair of scissors, Jim saying that he would keep his beard even on release to tease his mother. (He tells me that he did!)

The minders were obviously keen to keep us alive. After the initial supply of blood pressure tablets for me, Tom had requested tablets for excess stomach acid and general acid relief. These were supplied. Tom then went on to ask for Valium tablets to help him to sleep. When these were provided he sometimes took two a day which seemed to make him considerably more vocal and extrovert. This was a surprise and not the usual effect of Valium.

I had a worrying period over Christmas when I developed lumps in my right thigh. I self-diagnosed this as cellulitus, a condition I had had before. When it became clear that the lumps were not dissolving and there were signs of reddening in surface veins I asked for antibiotics. A box of Ciprofloxacin arrived after a few days. I took a course over ten days and the condition in my leg slowly improved. The minders would quite happily sample any of the tablets to show us they were harmless. All the medicines originated from countries like Cyprus and had directions and contraindications in English. The print was very small and I always asked Harmeet to read it out for me.

Jim was very fastidious about things like food and toilet hygiene. In spite of this, it was Jim who suffered from a cold and then came down with a fever. This was associated with nodules in his neck. At our suggestion Medicine Man came in with a digital thermometer. Paracetamol tablets and two sets of antibiotics were supplied. Jim wanted a particular type of antibiotic for what he assumed was a recurrence of the atypical pneumonia he had suffered in Canada. He suggested making a call to his doctor in Toronto, but that request was denied. He had to make do with the tablets provided. The fever raged for three days and we arranged for Jim to sleep on the futon during the day. He spent much of the time soaked in sweat, but the fever eventually left him. I knew Jim was better when he started to take charge again.

It was with Junior that the worst incident occurred, after Jim's fever. When he was sufficiently recovered to sit with us on the seats Junior came upstairs and stood in front us. Harmeet, he indicated, was always in a good mood while I, the doctor, and Jim were miserable. Jim was furious and must have come close to hitting Junior: 'Don't you tell me how I should feel!' Junior was taken aback. The incident was reported to Medicine Man, who came specially to sort things out, but Jim had already partially apologised for his outburst.

While Jim was still ill Medicine Man brought in some unidentified tablets for us all. He said 'These will do you good. Everybody takes them!' We declined.

During the second half of March Jim became concerned because my ankles started swelling. I thought, in my usual hypochondriac manner, that my cellulitus was returning. I started to take an antibiotic that Jim had not used during his bout of fever. Fortunately the SAS were responsible for preventing me finishing this course of unnecessary treatment.

Whenever Medicine Man appeared, we tried to engage him in some conversation. It must have been early in March that he told us how dangerous it was for him to keep us in this house. He felt that the security forces were closing in on his group of Mujahideen. One of their leaders had already been arrested. We offered Medicine Man very simple advice on how to avoid these dangers! He failed to take it.

12

WHAT WE DIDN'T KNOW

What do you do when 'the sky falls in'?
Sermon title: Revd Bob Gardiner

For this chapter I have relied on the recollections of Greg
Rollins of CPT, to whom I am grateful; on newspaper reports
and on the memory and records of my wife and family. The
recollections of my minister, the Revd Bob Gardiner, were
especially helpful and I also drew on the records of the Baptist
Union in Britain and the London support group.

Baghdad

My last sight of our driver and translator had been two figures
standing at the roadside. It was possible to piece together some
of what happened afterwards.

Greg Rollins at the CPT apartment in Baghdad received
a phone call from the translator to tell him that kidnappers
had abducted us. At first Greg thought it was a joke. When he
realised the translator was serious, he told the team and went
straight to work.

Greg described the next two weeks as a blur of non-stop
activity and sleepless nights – making phone calls, giving
interviews, writing releases, holding frequent team meetings,

consulting with advisors and making major decisions under enormous pressure. The team didn't have time to cook so the neighbours brought them dinner.

From both inside and outside Iraq, friends and strangers offered help and urged our release. The remarkable outpouring of support was very encouraging to the team and did a lot to dispel certain stereotypes about Muslim/Christian relations.

Believing the kidnappers might watch the CPT website, Greg posted messages to them. Iraqi friends advised him to address the kidnappers as 'brothers holding our colleagues'. They told him that this was considered respectful in Iraq. Greg was amazed. He had never imagined writing to kidnappers, let alone calling them his brothers!

The hardest part was the waiting. After early December the video statements from the kidnappers stopped and there were also fewer statements of support. As the weeks wore on, the team decided to get back into more of their regular work. More CPT members joined the team in the apartment, and at the request of Iraqi human rights groups they resumed the work of escorting Iraqis who were in danger, listening to people's stories and connecting with Iraqi peace groups.

A British perspective

While we were in captivity and during our times of worship we were sure that many people were praying for us and giving support to our relatives. We were, however, quite unaware of the scale and breadth of that support, both for our relatives and in public statements calling for our release.

On Saturday 26 November Pat was running a stall at our church Advent Fair. Our minister Bob Gardiner had been receiving my e-mails. During the Fair he handed Pat the one that I had sent on Friday 24:

Still safe in Baghdad – although we do hear about one bang a day plus police shooting in the air as they run through a convoy. We feel safe in the local area where the CPT are well known. However there is a lot of hanging about waiting for visits and I count the days to next Thursday when I fly back to Amman at 3.30 pm. Hope you have a great Fair!

Greetings and love,

Norman

Pat and Bob came to the (wrong) conclusion that I must have been feeling very frustrated if the mission had become a matter of counting the days!

At teatime Pat's phone rang. It was the CPT office in Chicago. The news was dire. The delegation had been kidnapped. Nobody was to use the word 'hostage' and nobody must know that we had been taken. CPT had decided to delay official news of our capture in the expectation that a reading of the magic sheet explaining why we were in Baghdad would prompt our captors to release us immediately. They feared that any intervention from the police or from authorities connected with the Coalition forces might stop that process.

Pat rang Bob Gardiner and his wife Tina came straight over to spend the night with her. Bob sat down to thrash out his advent sermon. It was to be based on the set readings for advent: 'O that you would tear open the heavens and come down' (Isaiah 64:1–9) and 'what do you do when the sky falls in?' (Mark 13:24–37). He decided to preach on the latter.

Bob recounts that the sermon was to be the keynote of the church's thinking and praying for the next four months. When the sky falls in it is only to bring the presence of God more obviously into our experience, carved out of the loneliness of the night's silent vigil. For most of that evening and night Bob worked and then reworked his material, with the TV tuned to 24-hour news channels. No one seemed to be saying anything. CPT were insistent that they would solve the matter and the British government was not to get involved. Bob was deeply unhappy about this and early next morning tried to get guidance from CPT about whom he could tell. The burden was too great to carry alone with Pat.

Eventually it was agreed that he would be allowed to tell a few friends and the church officers in the vestry before the morning service that there was a problem in Iraq involving CPT and that in the uncertainty they were to pray for Pat.

Pat went to Bob and Tina for Sunday lunch. That had been fixed before I left. I understand she spent most of the day in denial. The media remained silent but our daughters Sally and Joanna would have to be told. Pat rang them when she got home.

One curious incident is worth recounting; the strange story of the dog that didn't bark – or even move. My younger daughter Joanna and her husband Ian have a border collie, Josh. When the news of my capture reached their household the dog became silent and would not move from his position lying on the floor. This state of immobility continued overnight. The vet confirmed that there was no physical reason for the dog's depressed state.

My elder daughter Sally and her husband Maha were the first to arrive at our house, and made many further visits during the three-and-a-half months of captivity. At 6.00 pm the news broke that a Briton in Iraq had been taken hostage. Two hours later everyone knew it was me.

My younger daughter Joanna was given leave from her

teaching post and with her husband and our three-year-old grandson stayed with Pat until just before Christmas, when they all travelled home to Weymouth. We worked out that in their further trips during my captivity they covered 7,000 miles between Weymouth and Pinner.

Pat's brother John Cartwright and sister-in-law Miriam provided regular support with meals and diverting trips to London. My brother Ian and his wife Sheila came to stay. Pat visited them in Taunton and she was about to make a second visit when the news of my release broke. Other relatives supported Pat by letter, and her friends Helen Dunbar and Frankie Duffy were constant visitors. Friends and family were able to act as a vital shield against pictures and news that would cause Pat additional distress by censoring reports in newspapers and on television.

Following the announcement of my capture, crowds of media people gathered outside our home, making Pat a virtual kidnap victim herself. At one stage Pat counted fourteen cameras, and had to pull the curtains to keep the long lenses out. On the Monday she managed to break through the press cordon to get to a hospital appointment. Her friend Helen picked her up and drove away with a police car blocking the end of the road to prevent the media from following them. Pat shouted to the cameramen, 'You are making me a hostage in my own home!' After two days the police apparently told the cameramen to leave.

The antics of the press and TV crews would warrant a chapter of their own. Within two days the press had discovered the address of my daughter Joanna in Weymouth. She tells me that on the Monday after the kidnap reporters appeared at the school where she teaches at Puddletown in Dorset seeking interviews and pictures, although she managed to avoid them and made her way to London. They sought contacts among the lifeboat crew because my son-in-law Ian Thomas is a crew member – an immediate local focus of interest.

At one stage there were reporters at each end of the terrace where the family live but they did not know that their quarry could escape because there was a third way out of the house. Ian eventually made an agreement with the local paper, the *Dorset Echo*, that they would leave the family alone if he sent them a weekly email updating them on the current situation. My brother in Taunton also had visits from the press and TV at the time of my capture and again when I was released but disappointed them, as did the rest of the family, by his reluctance to seek passing fame on the telly.

But the media did play an important role. While they seemed a considerable nuisance at the time with their doorstepping of all who knew me and the initial besieging of Pat in our home, they did keep the story in the public eye and reported the events in generally positive terms. This reporting through a wide range of papers and radio stations meant that Pat had cards and letters from many members of the general public. These people were often unknown to us but shared Pat's concern. There were a few items of 'hate' mail, generally written in capitals with green ink and rarely with a signature. Such items were less than 1 per cent of the total, but were seized on by one newspaper as a suitable topic for a headlined article. I give a single example of the many positive letters – this from someone previously unknown to us.

Enfield, Middlesex
4 December 2005

Dear Mrs Kember
I am sure that this will be one of many letters you receive expressing both admiration and also concern for your husband. I heard part of the interview

he gave on Premier Radio (Armistice Sunday) and have also read about him in the newspapers. It is always so encouraging and inspiring to hear about people who not only hold such strong beliefs but are ready to live by them. It has such a very powerful effect and your husband's courage and his care for others simply reminds us all of the important things and what we should really value in life.

I, and many people I know, have been thinking of and praying for your husband and for you and your family. On Wednesday our Church, Trinity Methodist Church in Enfield town, will be open between 4.00 and 7.00 pm so that people can come in and pray together for your husband and his fellow hostages. A lot of the shops and businesses in Enfield have put notices in their windows advertising the fact that the church will be open. So many people are thinking of and praying for you and your husband and for all your family. I hope that you will draw some strength from knowing the love and support in prayer that comes to you all.

Cards and letters arrived from so many people we had known in the past; students I had taught, teaching and research colleagues, friends from my days at college in Exeter and Pat's teaching colleagues, as well as our neighbours in Pinner and Harrow. Pat was overwhelmed by gifts of flowers and particularly touched by the letters, pictures and even gifts sent by children – often from a whole class. The schools included a Muslim Saturday School.

Each morning the postman would knock to deliver a bundle of cards and letters. When he was in Pinner, three-year-old Ben would sit and open the letters and hand the

Some of the many cards Pat received from well-wishers

contents on to his Grandma – too often separating a card from the envelope with the address of the sender. Altogether about a thousand cards and letters were received – too many for personal replies.

Engineers arrived to set up a telephone monitoring system in case any calls came from Baghdad. For Pat's safety, she was given a panic button that was linked to the local police station. One day Pat, Joanna and Ben went for a walk, unaware that as they were leaving the house Ben had found the panic button. About ten minutes into their walk they heard in the background the wailing of sirens and wondered if there had been a traffic accident. On their return an hour later the next-door neighbour came to tell them what had happened. Three police cars had descended on the house, sirens wailing. Police had crashed through the side gate to gain entry to the garden and were getting ready to force their way through the front door when the neighbour intervened with a spare key. Pat apologised to the authorities and made a point of keeping the panic button well out of Ben's reach.

The police also provided Family Liaison Officers who were available to Pat 24 hours a day. They mediated the news to her and kept intrusive reporters at bay. These liaison officers became Pat's friends and she, in turn, provided them with a goodly supply of cups of tea. My son-in-law Ian formed a good relationship with the FLOs, with CPT in America and with the Foreign Office. The FLOs would contact him by mobile phone to pass on news – this happened once in a Tesco supermarket and once in the queue for meatballs in the Ikea café.

Ian's skill at surfing the net meant that sometimes he discovered news items before anyone else in the UK. His list of website contacts includes those from all parts of the globe although one site, JAWA, proved the most useful. He set up a banner heading on his own website which he uses to sell sign-writing projects on eBay. This banner was linked to an internet petition for our release which was promoted by 48 sponsors including Noam Chomsky, one of America's most prominent political dissidents, Denis Halliday, the former United Nations Humanitarian Coordinator in Baghdad and Milan Rai, the founder of Justice Not Vengeance. By Christmas it had been signed by more than 12,000 people.

Senior members of the Baptist denomination, including the London Regional Minister Pat Took, came to visit and pray with Pat. David Coffey, the General Secretary contacted Bob Gardiner to offer the expertise of their Press Officer Amanda Allchorn. Amanda made helpful contacts with the Foreign Office Press Officer and arranged media interviews with Bob and others.

Our own church was magnificent. Bob and Tina Gardiner could not have been more supportive. Bob was a wise counsellor, receiving and monitoring many messages throughout the period of captivity. He also took Pat on diverting trips to exhibitions in London. The church members, with 'Shaggy' (Elaine Abdon-Shortley), the pastoral worker, were very understanding and offered their assistance in quiet ways that did not distress Pat. She was invited to meals to ensure that she had company when the family was not present.

For the first month prayer vigils were held every day at the church. People signed up on a rota so that the church could be open all day, every day. Candles were lit and then a LED 'flame' put in the doorway of the church so that a light of hope would always be on view. Bob provided a book in which people could enter their prayers and comments. After Christmas the vigils were held on a weekly basis. Bob told me that, alongside their deep concern, they felt riddled with guilt, asking themselves, 'Why Norman?' 'Why did we not stop him going?' When it came to light that the Coalition (including the fledgling Iraqi government) were holding around 20,000 Iraqi prisoners, the Church added these prisoners to their prayers.

The wider Baptist family in Britain took up the commitment of regular prayers for us; they lit candles and arranged and attended vigils. Pat also had letters and cards from Italy, Australia, the USA, Chile and the European Baptist seminary in Prague. The full extent of the world-wide circle of prayer is still not known to us.

Other denominations joined in prayer vigils, and foremost were the Christian peace groups with whom I had connections. A support group met regularly to plan prayer vigils and press campaigns to explain the reasons for our mission to Baghdad. It was composed of Pat Gaffney of Pax Christi,

Chris Cole of the Fellowship of Reconciliation, Bruce Kent and Valerie Flessati of the Movement for the Abolition of War, Steve Whiting of Quaker Peace and Social Witness, Tim Nafziger of CPT and Ann van Staveren of the Council of Churches for Britain and Ireland.

Vigils were a major feature of the campaign in Britain. In London there was a weekly vigil in Trafalgar Square attended by a wide range of people. Muslims and Christians prayed together on the steps of St Martin-in-the-Fields and outside the National Gallery. Their prayers broadened to include CPT, the Muslim Association of Great Britain and their contacts in Iraq. They prayed for the kidnappers and their families and communities; for the Iraqi prisoners; for the Special forces, the Iraqi police and any others who might be involved in a rescue attempt, and also for the business people from Arab states who were beginning to offer ransom money. This continued through the bitterly cold weather of January and February. There were vigils in Oxford, Cambridge, Peterborough, Derby, Nottingham, Leicester, Bradford, Evesham, Malvern, Southampton and many other places. We also know of vigils held in Italy by Baptists and by Roman Catholics.

The secular press was apparently surprised by the strength of the support for us in all denominations, while the religious press printed regular articles on the captives and their motives for being in Iraq with the CPT. Pat received weekly phone calls from the CPT office in Chicago to exchange news while other members of CPT made calls of support. All calls to our number were monitored either by the family or by the police Family Liaison Officers.

The support of the Muslim community in Harrow and throughout Britain was extremely important. On 1 December, six days after we had been taken, a former President of the Muslim Association of Britain, Anas Altikriti, flew to Baghdad to try to secure our release. He had been born in Iraq and used his local knowledge to seek out any information on the kidnappers and to plead on our behalf. He reassured the people of Iraq that we were their friends and not in any way connected with the Coalition forces. His advocacy played an important part in keeping us alive by making it clear that we were people of peace. He was able to bring back assurances that we were still alive. That day the Arabic language television channel, Al Jazeera ran an impressive appeal by Palestinian Muslims for our release.

The day after the departure of Anas Altikriti, a video of the hostages was released and shown on Al Jazeera. In it we asked for the kidnappers' demands to be met; release of prisoners and our own release. The kidnappers' contribution was the threat that we would be killed if all Iraqi detainees were not freed by 8 December. On 2 December vigils were held in Trafalgar Square, Bradford, Oxford and Evesham.

The following day the Muslim Association of Britain published a remarkable letter. It was signed by Muslim leaders from Lebanon (including Hezbollah), Iraq, Palestine (including Hamas), Malaysia, Kashmir, Saudi Arabia, Yemen, Bahrain, Pakistan, India, Jordan and Algeria and called for our release. That such a wide range of Muslim groups made pleas for our release is remarkable. The full text is quoted as an appendix and in the final paragraph they called for our release in the strongest terms.

> While fully supporting the right of the Iraqi people to resist occupation with all legitimate means, we denounce as illegitimate any act of aggression against innocent civilians irrespective of their religion or nationality. We therefore call for the immediate release of these four hostages and of all other Western civilians kidnapped in

Iraq, and urge whoever has the ability to play a role in the endeavour to secure their release and their safe return to their countries to spare no effort in this regard. All illegitimate acts of aggression against innocent civilians, including kidnappings, indiscriminate killing or other forms of harm inflicted upon non-combatants, only harm the just cause of the Iraqi people and their legitimate struggle for freedom and independence.

On 6 December Abu Qatada, one of Britain's highest profile international terror suspects, issued a video appeal for our release from his prison cell in York. The following day this was shown on Al Jazeera. On Thursday 8 December a third video of the hostages was aired on Al Jazeera, showing only Tom Fox and me dressed in the Guantánamo Bay-style orange jumpsuits, blindfolded and shackled. We asked our respective governments to work for our release and that of the Iraqi people from oppression. It was announced on Al Jazeera that our kidnappers had extended their deadline from Thursday 8 to Saturday 10 December. On that same Thursday, former British prisoner of the US at Guantánamo Bay Moazzam Begg told BBC TV's *Newsnight* that seeing us in our orange jumpsuits on the video reminded him of his ordeal at the US base in Cuba.

On Friday 9 December the President of the banned Muslim Brotherhood in Egypt stated on Al Jazeera:

Islam rejects the kidnapping of innocent people regardless of their aim, beliefs and opinion. All laws locally and internationally consider kidnapping a crime, particularly when it targets innocent peace activists.

Prayers were said for us in many mosques of all the strands of Islamic belief.

Saturday 10 December was the deadline – midnight Baghdad time was 9.00 pm in London. An hour-long silent vigil was held in Trafalgar Square and a further vigil at Harrow Civic Centre. Afterwards Bob and Tina Gardiner came to sit with Pat and family members. There was no news. Bob left to prepare the children's Christmas service the following day, in which I had always played a part as secretary of the Sunday school. It was agreed that if bad news came through the service would be changed to reflect the mood.

On 12 December vigils were held in Trafalgar Square, Leicester, Derby and Oxford. On 13 December Al Jazeera reported that they had been inundated with emails and phone calls urging our release.

On Sunday 18 December David Coffey, General Secretary of the Baptist Union joined the congregation at Harrow Baptist Church. He brought a greeting from the Presidents of Churches Together in Britain and Ireland which he presented to Pat. The signatures on the card are those of Archbishop Rowan Williams, Cardinal Cormac Murphy-O'Connor, Bishop Nathan Hovhannisian, Primate of the Armenian Church of Great Britain and the Revd David Coffey as Moderator of the Free Churches. On 24 December the families of all the captives began placing advertisements in Iraqi newspapers and on radio stations calling for our release.

Pat had decided to spend Christmas with the family in Weymouth. With three-year-old Ben in the house Christmas had to be a celebration. Ben thought that I was away on an extended holiday, although he realised the strain my absence was putting on the adults in the family. One morning he joined his Grandma in bed. Hearing an aeroplane passing overhead he said, 'Granddad is in that plane and he'll come

Family appeal for hostages

A month has now passed since our loved ones - Norman, James, Harmeet and Tom - were kidnapped in Iraq.

They are all campaigners for peace. They are here in Iraq to listen to the suffering of the Iraqi people and to help with the release of detainees.

Many clerics and religious figures from the Arab and Muslim world have spoken over the past weeks of the good work they were doing in Iraq and that their organisation have done in Palestine, and have called for their release.
We too appeal for their safe return to us.
If you have any information which can help, please call this number. You do not have to reveal your identity.

07901 911 977
email: familyappeal@yahoo.com

Our families' appeal for our release

knocking on the door, run up the stairs, put on his big pyjamas, get into bed and start to snore!' Although this speech brought Pat close to tears, Ben's innocent optimism played an important part in keeping up morale, especially over the Christmas period.

Every Christmas since our marriage in 1960 I had made Pat a different cardboard model to contain her presents from me instead of a stocking. The models have included a Treasure Island, a sleigh, a Christmas tree and the Weymouth town clock. The girls were always eager to know what Dad had made for Mum each year. This year was to be the exception.

A kidnap team had been set up at Scotland Yard to monitor intelligence coming from Baghdad. The Foreign Office also played a major role behind the scenes, having set up investigation teams in Baghdad and in London. A member of the Scotland Yard team visited Pat and the family over the first two weeks to explain the situation. He then left for Baghdad to work with the investigation already in progress at the British Embassy there.

Pat was taken on four trips to the Foreign Office and was accompanied either by Bob, Joanna or our son-in-law Ian. There they met the people in closest contact with the Embassy team in Baghdad who were working for my release. Details of the background to our release were never made known for fear of jeopardising any such future operation. Pat was aware only that both detailed intelligence and planning work were taking place. She was told, in confidence, of the progress being made in seeking out the kidnap house and in identifying the kidnap group. On the first visit there was a direct video link between Pat and the deputy British Ambassador in Baghdad. The Foreign Secretary, Jack Straw kept in contact by phone. When I was released he commented on TV that Pat was a woman of 'extraordinary fortitude'. The Foreign Office also advised Pat on the television broadcasts that she was asked to make for Al Jazeera, who came to our house to film. Pat made three recordings appealing for my release. The Foreign Office, with the FLOs, advised on writing the scripts so that each appeal was made with a different emphasis. It is of interest that our Baptist connections were not mentioned, maybe because of the links between Baptists in the USA and Bush's aggressive policies. Having only 40 seconds or a minute to make these statements meant that they were stressful times, and Pat recalls the one occasion she admitted to not being able to put much emotion into the delivery. 'Don't worry', said the woman producer, 'I'll be making the voice-over in Arabic and I'll add all the necessary emotion'. As I mentioned previously, those broadcasts were seen by the kidnappers, although Pat's pleas and those on behalf of Jim, Harmeet and Tom seemed to have no effect on their determination to keep hold of us.

Pat's contacts with the police Family Liaison Officers and the Scotland Yard team caused some friction with the CPT office, and also with some members of our own family who were worried lest such 'official' contacts compromised a 'pure' pacifist position. When it was thought that there might be a request for a ransom there was some discussion about the feasibility of raising a ransom, although this was known to be against CPT policy and would put future captives at risk. This possibility was thought through amid considerable controversy among members of my family, although Bob Gardiner said that love comes before money. It was given no further consideration when it was realised that the sum required would be in excess of a million pounds!

There were seven particularly bleak weeks from 10 December onwards when the deadline passed without any news of our condition. At the beginning of January news came through of a further kidnap victim, the American journalist Jill Carroll, who had been taken by another previously unknown group, the Brigades of Vengeance. She was released on 30 March.

Pat was beginning to come to terms with what had happened and was now able to resume her role as assistant secretary at the Church. Others stepped into my shoes to plug gaps in the church's mission by editing the magazine, managing the website and preparing for the Pentecost bicentenary exhibition. Perhaps others were challenged to take new responsibilities in the life of the church.

Until 28 January there was no evidence that the four of us were alive. On that date, a video by our captors dated 21 January was broadcast on Al Jazeera. This one showed the four of us standing against a wall. It was accompanied by a statement from our captors saying that this was the 'last chance' for the authorities to release all Iraqi prisoners. Failing that, we would be killed.

In response to that broadcast an open letter was released on our behalf, signed by a multi-faith list of 42 religious leaders. During the accompanying press conference on 6 February Anas Altikriti made the point that the hostages had not only united people of all faiths but they had achieved the unthinkable: 'They have united the Muslim community itself.' During the following week news came through of an Iraqi human rights group who had been demonstrating in Baghdad for our release.

On Saturday 4 March Baptist churches across the country held a vigil and the following day there was a vigil in Trafalgar Square to mark 100 days since we had been taken. On Sunday 4 March members of our church wrote prayers on paper doves and placed them on a large branch of lilac from Bob and Tina's garden. They remained in place until my return.

On 7 March a new video was broadcast showing Jim, Harmeet and myself, but no Tom Fox. Three days later news was received that Tom had been murdered. This was the lowest point for Pat and my friends and family. Pat reacted to

The 100 days' vigil in Trafalgar Square

One of the many pictures Pat received from children

Tom's death with both courage and with terror – having killed the American, would the Briton be next? She spent an evening with Bob Gardiner considering my funeral service, a process which Joanna thought was unnecessarily negative. It was at this time that Pat's hope was kept alive by the family, including my grandson, and the volume of letters and cards of support from all over the world.

13

'STORMIN' NORMAN'[*]

I do not believe that a lasting peace is achieved by armed force, but I pay tribute to their courage and thank those who played a part in my release.

Norman Kember, statement at
Heathrow airport

On Wednesday evening, 22 March 2006 we were taken downstairs to eat our usual basic meal and watch a DVD on the television. Junior and Nephew were the minders on duty. They selected the second part of *Troy*, although we had already seen the whole film on previous evenings. At 10.00 pm we agreed to ask to be taken upstairs to sleep. The routine was as usual with individual visits to the *hammam* – toilet and teeth cleaning. We were settled down for the night with my right wrist chained, but with sufficient slack for me to reach the *hammam*. Jim and Harmeet were handcuffed together and Jim's right ankle was padlocked to the second chain which was fixed to the door.

We slept. On this night I did not need to make the expedition to the *hammam*. I was outstandingly fortunate to have been soundly asleep at about 8.00 am. Had I heard the noise of the armoured convoy arriving outside I would have been

* Headline in the *Sun* newspaper on my release.

in an extreme state of panic. We knew that the minders had the weaponry to put up a strong resistance to any raid, and might have had orders to shoot us.

The first thing I was aware of was a loud call, '*Aled*', coming from below. I now think it was a warning, probably from Medicine Man, to any of the minders who might still be inside.

There was then a noise of breaking glass and the sound of heavy boots entering the house. The noises were consistent with searching the rooms below – booby traps were always a possibility. Then there were boots pounding up the staircase, men rushing about and bursting open the doors of the rooms on our floor, and booted feet running up to the floor above.

Jim called out to me to lie down, but I was already on my feet and looking through the gap in the door. I saw heavily-armed men in light khaki battledress and assumed that they were the Coalition forces, not another group of Mujahideen.

Men erupted into the room and a British voice said: 'Is Mr Kember here?' I don't know if I spoke out loud or simply nodded. Medicine Man seemed to be with the soldiers at this stage. One of the soldiers called for a pair of bolt cutters which made short work of the padlocks. I was freed of the chains and Jim and Harmeet were also released from their shackles.

I took off my hated light-blue track suit trousers with the tomato stains and put on my own brown trousers and my jacket from the top of the pile of chairs by the window. I filled my pockets with the packs of medicines from the top of the hostess trolley, took up my notebook and prepared to leave. I do regret that I forgot to grab the Wile E. Coyote mug!

Jim and Harmeet were also gathering their property. I remember Harmeet using a pillow case, while he recalls making a trip to the bathroom only to discover that the door had been smashed down. As we were bumbling around Jim turned to the soldiers and asked if they had news of Tom Fox.

'Yes,' said the soldiers. 'Tom Fox has been killed.'

'Are you sure?' said Jim.

They were sure. In a sad way the news did not really come as a shock. In spite of our captors' reassurances we had become increasingly certain that Tom must indeed be dead.

Together we were escorted down the stairs through the kitchen and out into the open air, and took our first breath of fresh air since arriving at the house more than three months ago. I noted the trees in the garden in front of the house. I saw Medicine Man standing facing the driveway wall, still in his nightshirt and with a blindfold over his eyes. I forbore to say anything to him. There was no sign of Junior or Nephew. They must have had warning of the raid.

Coming out of the front gates we realised that the house was on a main dual carriageway. Outside was a battle tank, two Bradley armoured personnel carriers and a row of Humvees (armoured descendants of the jeep). The convoy was apparently manned by American and British troops.

According to an independent eyewitness to our release, a large armoured convoy had arrived and sealed off the area. Householders were warned to stay indoors and shut all curtains. By peeping through a bedroom window this witness saw some people including an old man (that's me) and a person with long hair (that's Harmeet) leaving the house before the column moved off.

The two Canadians disappeared into the bowels of one of the Bradleys while I climbed into the front seat of a Humvee. I shook hands with the driver and the man sitting behind him introduced himself as a medic. He took out a pack of beta-blocker tablets for blood pressure and offered one to me with the comment that he had been carrying these with him for some weeks – hoping that he would have an opportunity such as this to use them.

After a few minutes the whole convoy moved off – the tank ploughed its way over the concrete kerb divider in the middle of the dual carriageway and all the other vehicles followed. I looked back at the house without any regret! I saw that there were a few shops nearby and across the road the entry booths to some sort of sporting stadium. I have now learned that the house was in the Al Mansour district of Baghdad and close to the Green Zone (see map p. 36).

I am ignorant of the details of the detective work that led to our release. It is possible to speculate at length on the events that led up to 23 March, but what follows is my understanding. There had been extensive enquiries which apparently led to a list of possible kidnappers.

I do not know how they came to discover Medicine Man but very early that morning there had been a raid on Medicine Man's house, which was in a well-to-do area of Baghdad. He was questioned but pretended only to understand Arabic. One of the interrogators said something to the effect of: 'He is of no use to us – take him outside'. That produced a change of language. Medicine Man admitted to knowing where we were. I believe that he led the armoured column, which must have been on stand-by for such an eventuality, to the house. A report in *The Times* suggested that a full assault on the house had been avoided. The minders had been warned to leave, so that one frail old man (that was me!) would not be subjected to the rigour of a full assault. There were certainly no deaths or injuries as a result of the raid – a condition that my family and the CPT had always sought.

So here I was, sitting in the front of a Humvee with a great view as we drove through the streets of Baghdad towards the Green Zone. The traffic had been cleared and was at a standstill on either side of the road. People on the roadsides watched as we wove our way through a few checkpoint barriers. In perhaps twenty minutes we entered the Green

Zone and my Humvee peeled away from the convoy. We drove into a cleared area with a helicopter and waited until Jim and Harmeet joined us, somewhat shaken by their trip in a noisy steel box. Then the officer in charge of the Special forces rescue team took us in hand and reminded us that our decision to take a risk in coming to Baghdad had involved risks for many other people, including the men under his command. We looked suitably admonished. This was certainly not the time to expound on CPT policy! Photographs were taken with the three of us standing with the soldiers involved.

We climbed into the helicopter and flew a short distance to a helicopter pad near the US Military Hospital. As we entered, members of staff were lined up to welcome us. I was taken to a bay where two nurses helped me to undress and slide under a blanket. A fluid drip was attached to my arm to take care of possible dehydration. Then the basic measurements were made – pulse, temperature, blood pressure and then an ECG. All were pronounced normal. A portable machine was wheeled in for a standard chest X-ray. It was known that I had a small aneurysm in my abdominal aortic artery so I was not surprised when an ultrasonic imager appeared. The sonographer applied the contact jelly to my abdomen to scan and measure my aorta and then made a thorough examination of my left leg in case there were signs of deep vein thrombosis. There were none.

Some further players appeared on the scene. There was the US Army chaplain who offered prayers of thanks and then suggested that I might have need of a Bible. I asked for a Good News version. More materially, I was also offered a cup of tea and, yes, a chocolate biscuit!

At some stage I was introduced to Adrian, a senior police officer who was to accompany me all the way to Heathrow. I was also provided with a basic outfit since all my clothes and other belongings had been taken off for forensic examination, including my captivity notebook. I was allowed to keep the cheese box that contained the games and one pair of baggy underpants.

From the US hospital we were conveyed to the staff club of the British Embassy. All our journeys took us alongside the high concrete walls that characterise the Green Zone. At each gap in the walls our identities were checked by the Gurkha soldiers on duty.

The Embassy staff club is a modern single-storey block, again enclosed behind high concrete walls. It has a large swimming pool and alongside it a recreation room with a range of easy chairs and an area of café-type chairs and tables. At one end of the room were a very large TV and a board showing the fixtures for forthcoming British soccer matches. At the other end was a well equipped bar.

Jim, Harmeet and I walked on the pool terrace in the sunshine. Dishes of sandwiches and cakes were brought into the bar and we were offered a range of drinks. We took them outside to sit at the tables on the terrace but I soon decided that the sun was too hot and retired to eat inside. By the afternoon, Jim had soaked up so much sun that his face had turned a bright shade of red.

Gordon, an officer in the Royal Canadian Mounted Police (the Canadian equivalent of my senior police officer Adrian) came to meet Jim and Harmeet, and the three of them went for a walk together outside the immediate concrete enclosure to an area of wasteland where there were a few trees.

Now was the time to phone Pat. I learned afterwards that Pat had been woken up by a phone call at 6.14 that morning (9:14 am Baghdad time) from the Family Liaison Officer. She had been planning to travel to Taunton that day, but was told to cancel the trip and that the FLO was coming round to see her within the next half hour. He did not say on the phone what the news was but hinted that it was not bad. Pat could only get up and await the visit. The FLO arrived shortly to tell her the great news: 'Norman's released. He will be phoning you. We have got to sit here and wait.'

In Baghdad we were each provided with a mobile phone on which to make calls. I had long ago decided that in such a wonderful event I might be too emotionally overcome to make sense. Adrian sat by me on a sofa and dialled the number. Pat answered. Adrian explained briefly who he was. He said that I was sitting next to him, that I was well and looking forward to seeing Pat again. I then took over the phone and managed a few words of greeting through my tears (my eyes grow moist as I type this recollection). I had to hand the phone back to Adrian, who said: 'Norman's fine. He'll speak to you again.' That was the first phone call.

I rejoined the others and a series of events followed (I cannot recollect the exact order). Some of our clothes and toilet things from the CPT flat had been delivered to the poolside. Clutching these items we were taken to prefabricated huts called pods, all protected by piles of sandbags. It was suggested we might stay the night here. In each pod were two rooms – in ours, Adrian was allocated one room and I the other. There were beds, a bathroom with a shower and furniture for clothes storage. A bag with toilet necessities was provided. I laid out my clothes, took a quick shower and started to remove the remains of my beard and moustache. At last I recognised myself in the mirror!

When we returned to the poolside, a member of the Embassy staff enquired whether there were items we wanted. I badly needed some shoes, since I only had a poorly fitting pair of hospital flip-flops, and a belt was also a necessity to hold up my trousers. Sunglasses and a hat were added to the list. These items appeared shortly afterwards, together with some ice-cream! My new shoes were a pair of white Nike trainers.

With the British Ambassador, Harmeet and Jim

Since I had lost my passport it was essential to have a replacement. I was duly photographed and equipped with a new emergency passport before I left Baghdad. I asked to be weighed and the scales showed a loss of about one-and-a-half stones in weight. My next book, *The Baghdad Diet,* should be a best-seller!

In the afternoon I made a second call to Pat. This time I managed without help and was able to tell Pat in a fairly firm voice that I expected to be home in one or two days. It was Thursday afternoon and a homecoming on Saturday 24 March was possible.

I only learned later of the intense media excitement at the news of our release. The Family Liaison Officers kept the reporters away from Pat but our church then became the centre of attention. The amazing news that I was free arrived at the church early during the Thursday coffee morning. Bob Gardiner writes, 'People literally danced in the aisles. Those with arthritis walked as they had not walked for years. There was singing of the doxology in the foyer, while I did 17 media interviews. TV crews queued to get into the church. The winter was over and spring had come big-time.'

Amanda Allchorn, the Baptist Union press officer, was quickly on hand to deal with the media and the church was able to celebrate the news in prayer and praise. A televised interview was arranged with officers of our church and of the Baptist Union. Amanda tells me that her phone rang constantly with calls from the media as well as from Christian groups and individuals who wanted to share in the rejoicing. The media also sought out other people like Alan Betteridge of the Baptist Peace Fellowship who knew me. Chris Cole of the Fellowship of Reconciliation found himself fought over by Sky News and BBC News 24 reporters until the latter group bundled him away to their cameras.

In Baghdad, the three of us at last met the CPT team again when they came into the Green Zone to see us at the Embassy. Maxine Nash, Anita David and Peggy Gish were among the current members of the team who had bravely remained in Baghdad for the entire period of our captivity. They brought the remainder of our belongings from the apartment so that I was reunited with a spare pair of reading glasses (at last!) and the rucksack and shoulder bag I had brought to Iraq. We exchanged warm hugs of welcome.

Jim and Harmeet went with the team to start a debriefing. After exchanging greetings I simply did not find myself able to say too much about how I was feeling so I went and took refuge in the Embassy staff lounge. In talking about this afterwards, Adrian and I agreed that the British are more diffident about expressing their emotions.

The next thing was a telephone call from the Foreign Secretary, Jack Straw. I fear that I made an incoherent and ungracious reply. I have now sent a more considered expression of gratitude to him and to the Foreign Office staff – to this Jack Straw replied with a hand-written letter.

In the evening I made a third phone call to Pat with my emotions under control and she tells me that we had a good conversation and that this time I sounded like me! I was able to reassure her that I was in good health and good spirits. I learned later that Pat had been concerned by the writing on the paper when I had responded to her three specific questions to prove I was still alive. My writing was so poor that Pat feared I might have had a stroke. It did not occur to her that I might be without my glasses.

The British Ambassador, Sir William Patey, arrived to greet us. He suggested that we might all be more comfortable sleeping in his residence. After making arrangements for a further meeting between the CPT staff and the Canadians the following day, the three of us collected our belongings from the pods and were driven through more concrete barriers to a large mansion.

It is difficult to describe this building – I had seen nothing like it in any of the National Trust properties I have visited. A spacious entrance hall led into a vast space under a domed ceiling. This space was crossed at an upper level by a bridging corridor which was reached by a curving staircase. Generous open spaces upstairs gave entry to the bedrooms. We were told that the house had been the residence of one of Saddam's mistresses.

Later that evening we had a meal prepared by the Ambassador's personal 'Man Friday'. We sat at a table made famous by Gertrude Bell, Oriental Secretary to the High Commissioner in Baghdad during the British mandate after the First World War. It was she who in 1922 had drawn in the

My luxurious room at the Ambassador's residence

borders of modern Iraq for the High Commissioner to present to Arab leaders. We were told that the map she used had rested on this very table. But we were more interested in the food – I seem to remember that there was soup, fish and ice cream. There was a television room and I watched some items of news about our release before sending an email of greetings to the CPT office in Chicago.

I had woken up that morning lying on a floor in chains. I went to sleep that evening in an enormous bed in the luxury of the Ambassador's residence.

14

HOMECOMING

In reality it was my wife who was kidnapped last November. She suffered more than I because while I knew that I was alive and well, she did not.
　　　　　　　　　　Norman Kember, statement
　　　　　　　　　　　　　　　on his release

Sleep deserted me for my night in the British Ambassador's residence, even though I had had the pleasure of going to bed in pyjamas with a cup of hot Horlicks for the first time in all those months. The room was comfortable but the air conditioning was rather noisy. After three months of trying to switch my brain off as much as possible, it leapt into action that night with every neural circuit fully functional.

I left the bed to walk about from time to time and look for reading matter. In the box that held the phone was an instruction booklet – here was a chance to crack the mysteries of mobile phones. The booklet was in Arabic. On a further peer into the box and I found a manual in English, but it might as well have been in Arabic!

At 6.00 am I drew myself a wonderful bath full of hot water and soaked in it for half an hour at least. Dressed, I went downstairs for breakfast. Joy! Cereal with milk and marmalade on toast. I seem to remember that Jim and Harmeet ate rather more of the cooked breakfast that was on offer. The

Canadian RCMP officer gave me two Mounties lapel badges and we learned in discussion that he and Adrian were part of an international network of hostage experts who pool their experience and knowledge.

The Ambassador told us that the press were anxious for some sort of bulletin from us. He suggested something simple and I just said that it was great to be free, that I had had a fair night's rest and had enjoyed a good breakfast. It was this brief bulletin that was seized upon as evidence that I had not thanked the British troops who released me. According to a report in *The Times* the rescue team have a photograph of them hugging us and that photograph was pinned to a noticeboard in their HQ. By coincidence, I later flew out of Baghdad with one of the soldiers who released us and we had a friendly exchange. He showed me the severed padlock which they had cut to release the chain that bound me to the door. It was to become an exhibit in the SAS collection of memorabilia.

After breakfast we visited the British Embassy and were able to thank, in person, the team who had worked so hard for our release. They applauded us but we, in turn, applauded them. We had little idea even at this time of the amount of investigative work that had been carried out by intelligence services in the lead up to our dramatic release.

It was arranged that I would be flown out to Baghdad airport at 1.00 pm. The two Canadians were to spend one more night in Baghdad before a Canadian aircraft was brought in to fly them to Dubai on the first stage of their journey home. Since this was to be our last time together we had a meeting in their bedroom (filled with Ikea furniture, much to Jim's chagrin!).

We went out onto the landing to sing Tom Fox's song:

If all the people lived their lives
as if it were a song into the light,
providing music for the stars
to dance their circles in the night.

It was our tribute to Tom.

We had lunch together and made our farewells, promising
to keep in touch, as we have done. Jim and Harmeet went to
prepare for a second debriefing session with the CPT team.
They were more prepared to talk about our ordeal than I was
at this time and perhaps prone to speculate a little about the
mystery surrounding the circumstances of our release.

Then began my wait for the final move out of Baghdad
that I had anticipated so hopefully over all those months. By
1.30 pm I was getting rather twitchy. The Ambassador sensed
this and a phone call from him ensured that we had a priority
place on the next helicopter leaving the Green Zone for the
airport.

That helicopter ride was hairy. The side door was open
and a machine gunner sat there in readiness to respond to any
attack. I was equipped with a flak jacket and helmet and
strapped into my seat. From time to time flares were fired off
to deflect any possible heat-seeking missiles. The flight was
perhaps only fifteen minutes long but it was a dramatic
experience.

At Baghdad airport the Ambassador and I waited in a
lounge in the US military area. Further passengers were
expected to arrive by helicopter after thirty minutes or so.
The Ambassador was also on his way to London and he and
I were led to the waiting Hercules aircraft and climbed up
into seats behind the pilots. Adrian disappeared into the
bowels of the plane. In fact I was given the best passenger seat,
slightly behind but between the two pilots. I was equipped

*A machine gunner at the open door of the helicopter during our
ride to Baghdad airport*

with earphones and mike so that I could follow their
communications and ask questions.

Unfortunately the day was cloudy and I saw very little of
the landscape from this advantageous position. But I was able
to watch the pilots handling the controls and listen to communications with ground control. It was not until the plane
had reached full height that we were allowed to remove our
flak jackets.

After about one-and-a-half hours I could just make out
islands in the Persian Gulf beneath us, and we shortly came in
to land at Kuwait airport. A car was waiting to drive Adrian
and me to the Kuwaiti Embassy and on this journey I was
under the care of one of the Embassy staff. The drive revealed
Kuwait to be as well-groomed as Baghdad was unkempt. The
roads were lined with grass verges and flowers. There were

villas and factories and hotels, all in sparkling condition. I saw no signs of the 1991 Gulf War.

The Embassy in Kuwait is a delightful building and one of the oldest in the city, although it dates only from the 1920s. The Ambassador's residence is on the first floor and has a long curving veranda overlooking a lovely garden with flowering shrubs and a fountain. Beyond the garden is a coast road and then the sea.

That afternoon I made a further phone call home to Pat. She told me that she was going to be taken to Heathrow airport for a reunion in one of the private lounges.

The details of the flight home the following day and the fact that there was to be a press conference at Heathrow were explained. It had been agreed that only the BBC and Reuters would be present, but their material was to be made available to all news sources. There would be no questions. Adrian handed me a list of topics that I might wish to cover in a press briefing but I said that I was quite capable of writing my own statement. I spent some time composing it in the early hours of Saturday morning. I based it on the ideas that I had jotted in my captivity notebook, and wrote it out as legibly as I could so that it could be typed for general circulation. I also wrote a note to the British Ambassador to Kuwait who was in London to thank him for the hospitality that his staff had offered.

It was in Kuwait that Adrian decided that my hair style was much too ragged to warrant an appearance before the British press. A box of hair clippers was produced and Adrian explained that he had had some experience as a barber in his service life. That is the story of my police haircut – not quite a shaven head but close to it. Adrian assured me that he had had to cut the hair short to remove the last evidence of my captors' jagged handiwork.

Adrian and I were entertained by a member of the

Embassy staff, Nicholas Watson and his wife Catriona. Over a meal we learned about the joys and trials of diplomatic life. The Watsons were shortly to be assigned to Saudi Arabia, where Catriona would not be allowed to drive her children to school but would have to depend on male drivers.

One aspect of my appearance was troubling me and I shared it with Nicholas and Catriona. The pair of white trainers with which I had been provided in Baghdad would have been fine for a half marathon but would hardly be a morale booster when exposed to TV cameras. I asked if there was a shoe shop at Kuwait airport and Nicholas said he would see what could be done.

That night I did get some sleep since the air conditioning was not required – the room was kept cool with a silent but effective ceiling fan. My room was on a corner of the building and when I did wake it was possible to explore the balconies at two sides of the room, both with sea views and one overlooking a small swimming pool. I was tempted to try a swim but was unsure of my physical condition.

On Saturday morning there were some newspapers on a table. Most were in Arabic, but I was able to read the news of our release in the one English paper. After breakfast Nicholas produced a fine pair of brown shoes to go with my brown trousers and fleece. He had won them at an embassy party and, not having worn them, was happy to hand them to a grateful recipient. A brief walk in the Embassy garden and we were off to the airport. We waited a little while in the VIP lounge where Adrian and I were joined by Sir William Patey from Baghdad, who had stayed in an hotel.

There was a delay due to the careful arrangements made to ensure that I would not be troubled by journalists. Only when all the rest of the passengers were in their places did we climb aboard the plane by the steps to the door at the front of the aircraft. I was welcomed by the cabin staff and seated in the front row with one of the British Airways security chiefs beside me. The Ambassador and Adrian sat in the row behind.

I was told that the CPT office in Chicago had leaked information about the flight I was to be on. There were in fact members of the press on the plane including a *Mail on Sunday* reporter just three rows behind me. My 'minders' kept him at bay.

On the individual TV screens I watched the maps showing the progress of the flight towards London – we flew over Baghdad! The cabin crew provided me with a tape of an early BBC 24 broadcast so that I was able to see reports of our release. There was a list of films that could be selected for viewing and among them was *Transporter 2* (so beloved of our captors). I did not watch it.

Although the food was excellent – I ate lobster – the best aspect of the flight was the opportunity to engage in some normal conversation. I had a long chat with the security chief from British Airways. We exchanged information about our families and he also gave me some insights into his job and told me that he had been on flights with many distinguished people including Nelson Mandela. Part of his job was to assess the risks of landing at various airports. Baghdad was still on the forbidden list.

From my seat I could easily walk into the stewards' galley, where they talked to me about their experiences. I remember that the senior steward has his home near Blackpool. Another steward was French, but she preferred working for BA to the rather regimented Air France. I was also able to have brief talks with the pilot and co-pilot as they came into the galley. I must record that before I left the aircraft the crew presented me with a bottle of champagne and a bottle of Chanel No. 5 perfume for my wife.

As we flew across Europe there were some glimpses of the

topography below but it was generally a cloudy day. I did see the English Channel and recall that we first flew over British soil somewhere north of Southend-on-Sea. The landing was smooth and there we were, back at Heathrow. After a long phase of taxiing we came into the designated berth and then, leaving the plane, descended to a waiting car that transferred us to a VIP lounge suite.

I knew that Pat would be there to meet me as two Family Liaison Officers had brought her with my younger daughter to the airport. I walked into the private room in which Pat and Joanna were waiting. I had feared that I would be overcome with emotion, but Pat and I gave each other one large hug and then I was able to talk to her and to Joanna without tears. I reassured them that I was in good spirits and in good health. There was no time to discover what had been happening at home, although they told me that my elder daughter Sally would be waiting for me in Pinner.

We discussed the statement that I was to make – Pat had been provided with a script in case I was not up to delivering it myself. After ten minutes or so we were taken next door into the room where a television camera was set up and reporters from Reuters and the BBC were waiting. I sat on a sofa with Pat and read out the prepared statement.

To ease the atmosphere I decided to preface the reading with an inquiry about the *Sun* newspaper reporter who had dreamt up the headline 'Stormin' Norman'. After this television session I was delighted to be introduced to members of the police and Foreign Office staff who had played such a vital role in supporting Pat and working for our release.

I had been warned that the photographers who have access passes to most parts of Heathrow would be waiting and we walked out of the VIP lounge into a barrage of flashes. We were driven away in one car and then changed to another to throw the media off the scent. I believe that the car in which

Joyful reunion at Heathrow airport
(Luke MacGregor-Pool/Getty Images)

we finally left the airport had a marking on the roof that enabled the Sky News helicopter to follow us easily. The pilot must have wondered what we were up to since we found ourselves on the road towards Terminal 5 instead of making for Pinner. Having recovered from that slight mistake our driver recalled the correct route away from Heathrow.

I was woefully unprepared for the intense media interest in my release and return. There were continuous news reports on BBC News 24 and on other satellite channels. Many of my friends told us that they sat glued to their screens all day.

Television and radio journalists had a challenging time broadcasting with so little factual detail. At one time they accepted a rumour that I was going straight to our church!

The reporters were assisted by a wide circle of contacts in the peace movement including my support group: Pat Gaffney of Pax Christi, Chris Cole of the Fellowship of Reconciliation, Bruce Kent and Valerie Flessati of the Movement for the Abolition of War, Steve Whiting of Quaker Peace and Social Witness, Tim Nafziger of CPT and Ann van Staveren of Council of Churches for Britain and Ireland.

David Cockburn of CPT UK had a busy day providing background information about peacemaking for TV channels and the press. Jonathan Bartley of Ekklesia was also active. This Christian media service had kept up a full report on our captivity on their website. These friends noted the change in media attitude from supportive to critical after General Sir Michael Jackson had alleged my lack of gratitude to his soldiers. They had to spend time countering that accusation and pointing out the positive reasons for my trip to Iraq.

The scene as we arrived at our road was amazing. The first part of the street was nearly blocked with TV vans and cars. The neighbours were out in their front gardens and as we drove nearer to our house the crowd increased with newspaper and TV photographers and reporters. The police had brought in crush barriers for the pavements and they made room for us to stop outside the house. As we got out the photography started. I gave a brief wave to acknowledge the applause of the friends who had gathered and walked through our front gate. I was aware that our neighbour was in the next garden. I reached through the hedge to shake his hand, and that was it – through the front door and into our home. My grandson Ben peeped through the curtains from time to time and the waiting photographers had to be satisfied with shots of him.

Ben watching at the window as I arrive home
(Andrew Stuart/AFP/Getty Images)

My elder daughter, Sally and her husband Maha had travelled up from Portsmouth to welcome me. In addition to my younger daughter, Joanna, son-in-law Ian and grandson, Ben, there was Pat's brother, John Cartwright and her sister-in-law, Miriam. We also had two Family Liaison Officers present. It was quite a house-full. I exchanged greetings with them all and thanked them for caring for Pat during this traumatic time. John and Miriam provided a celebration cake and a bottle of champagne. And in all the rooms there was a wonderful display of flowers and greeting cards.

I had the opportunity to ask Sally about her change of career from engineer to therapy radiographer and inquired about Maha's projects to develop energy-saving housing. I fear that I then escaped outside to look at the garden and it was here that I gave the Sky News helicopter the opportunity for a candid camera shot. Ben was intrigued by the police presence and chatted to the officers on duty in our back garden.

The FLOs and family members took their leave and for that first evening Pat and I were left alone – that is, without counting the media pack outside. For the rest of that day and for the next two days we kept the curtains pulled at the front of the house and the police vetted anyone who approached the front door. Bob Gardiner and Tina did call later that evening and we discussed whether I would cause too much distraction if I came to Morning Service the next day. Media or no media, if I was not free to attend church I was not really free! I decided to attend.

To sleep in the familiar bed was a great pleasure. I slept well but got up early to check up on my computer. The email inbox had filled up with spam so that it had not been able to receive new emails. After breakfast – shredded wheat and all-bran with toast and marmalade – I prepared for our outing to church.

The media photographers were still lined up across the street from our house. A friend drove up to our front gate to pick us up and the police cleared a passage for us to join her. They also prevented the press from following the car but the media were already at the church in strength. A parking space was reserved for us at the side of the church and the photographers came running when they realised who was in the car. We were admitted through a side door and went upstairs to wait in the church office until the service was ready to

begin. We then made our way into the organ loft which over-
looks the church so that we were able to hear the opening of
the service.

During the first hymn we entered the church through the
rear door and took our places in seats at the back. Our
minister had already asked the congregation not to crowd us
and there were few heads that turned.

Amanda Allchorn had made an agreement for a pooled
television presence at the service and two cameras were in
position within the church to do the necessary filming. They
spent too much time focussing on me and not enough on the
worship. It was at this service that a message of welcome and
thanksgiving from Shahid Akmal of Harrow mosque to Bob
Gardiner was read out:

> We are grateful to Allah for His mercy that
> Norman Kember has safely returned home to be
> re-united with his family and friends and I write
> to pass on our delight at this wonderful news. The
> past few months must have been very difficult for
> Norman's wife, Pat, and their family. We have
> watched how Pat has conducted herself so grace-
> fully and were touched that in his welcome back
> speech, Norman specifically remembered the
> victims of the conflict now raging in Iraq and
> found words to still speak out against all forms of
> violence. We give thanks for the release of
> Norman's other colleagues James Loney and
> Harmeet Singh Sooden too. Of course we
> remember with much sadness the needless loss of
> Tom Fox and the countless other innocents who
> have perished in this conflict.
>   On behalf of the Muslims of Harrow, my fel-
> low Mosque Executive Members and our Imams,

we too welcome Norman back to our community of Harrow. He is truly an example to us all and we pray that his experience, difficult and distasteful though it must have been, will have served to strengthen his resolve to continue his work for peace in the world. We are proud to stand with him in this. He epitomises the verse of the Qur'an which states: 'Closest to the Believers (Muslims) will you find those who say: "We are Christians". For among them are men of learning, men who renounce the world and men who are not arrogant or proud.'

At the front of the church I saw the branch of the tree on which paper doves had been fixed and during the service I was given the book of messages that had been recorded at prayer vigils and other services. This book together with the cards and letters are a constant reminder to me of the support that I had from ordinary people during the captivity.

After the service it was suggested that we give the media a photo opportunity and Pat and I walked together down the front drive of the church while the cameras flashed. It was with these happy images that the newspapers were provided their front page pictures on the Monday.

Drawing and letter from a child in Pennsylvania

The handwritten statement I read out at London Heathrow on Saturday 25 March 2006

Before reading the prepared statement I asked if the reporter who dreamt up the headline 'Stormin' Norman' for the Sun *was present.*

There is a real sense in which you are interviewing the wrong person. It is the ordinary people of Iraq that you should be talking to – the people who have suffered so much over many years and still await the stable and just society that they deserve.

Another group that I hope you do not forget are the relatives of British soldiers killed or wounded in Iraq.

I do not believe that a lasting peace is achieved by armed force, but I pay tribute to their courage and thank those who played a part in my release.

I am not ready at this time to talk about my months of captivity except to say that I am delighted to be free and reunited with my family.

In reality it was my wife who was kidnapped last November. She suffered more than I because while I knew that I was alive and well, she did not. I thank all who supported Pat during this stressful time.

While in Baghdad we had opportunity to thank the Embassy staff who worked so diligently for our release. I now thank the staff in Britain who also dedicated so much time to the same end.

Then I am grateful to all those from many faith communities who appealed for my release and held prayers and vigils in my name.

Pat assures me that I will be overwhelmed by the volume of goodwill messages – our home is currently like a flower shop.

I thank the media for agreeing to share news and reduce the stress on me.

I now need to reflect on my experience – was I foolhardy or rational? – and also to enjoy freedom in peace and quiet.

Thank you.

15

REFLECTIONS

*Please do not wish the ungrateful and arrogant
Kember on us. We are already well up to quota on
do-gooders, nutters and holier-that-thou bigots,
thank you, without more being shipped in.*

In going to Iraq was I foolish or rational?

Insofar as Christian Peacemaker Teams are about taking risks
as peacemakers, I was obeying an inner urge to be true to my
Christian beliefs. In Paul's letters in the New Testament he
talks about the Christian faith being foolishness. In the eyes
of the world, Jesus' way of life was foolish, for example taking
risks in trusting people and challenging those in power.
Hence there is a long tradition in Christianity of being fools
for the sake of Christ in the manner of Dostoevsky's *The Idiot*.
I admit to being foolish in that sense.

I also consider that one should not take unreasonable risks.
Two weeks before I left for Iraq, the CPT office sent me a
letter reminding me of the dangers. At that point I did quite
seriously consider backing out. On the other hand we are
told in the New Testament that 'He who puts his hand to the
plough and turns back is not worthy of the Kingdom' (Luke

9:62). Rather more mundanely, I had told many people that I was off to Iraq so it was also a matter of pride. Irresponsibly, I had not checked up on the dangers by logging on to the internet to read the risks of travel to Iraq detailed on the Foreign Office website. Would further knowledge of the risks have produced a change of mind?

There is another aspect. If I had known the anguish I would cause my wife, I would not have gone. When people ask if I am going back to Baghdad I answer, 'When my wife allows me!'

Shortly after our release, CPT withdrew their team from Iraq because of a general feeling that the security situation in Baghdad had so far deteriorated that all CPT staff were at risk. They have now sent some team members back to Iraq, but not to Baghdad, because their Iraqi contacts requested that they return. The question arises: are CPT putting the lives of others at unnecessary risk?

One can argue that lifeboat crews and other volunteer rescue workers put their own lives at risk as a result of the decisions of others to pursue leisure activities in a manner that is sometimes rash or ill advised, and not even in the cause of peacemaking.

If future CPT delegates or members in Iraq are kidnapped, are CPT responsible for putting the lives of soldiers at risk because government and military authorities feel obliged to seek out captives in order to release them? The standard CPT answer is that they did not ask the SAS to put their lives in danger to free hostages. It was a choice made by the relevant governments. CPT also makes the point that soldiers know the risks they take when they sign up for special duties. Personally, I do not find this answer altogether satisfactory.

How do I reconcile the dilemma that I came in peace and went out with the SAS?

I am continually thankful for being rescued by the SAS. I did not refuse to be released when they came storming up the stairs, neither did I object to being conveyed out of captivity in military vehicles, helicopters and planes. I admit to being inconsistent – and human.

I cannot make a full reconciliation of this dilemma and have to accept this as an irony of life! However the point can be made that in recent times the army have on occasion taken on a role as peacemakers. British army officers have been sent on courses in conflict resolution by peaceful means at the Bradford University Department of Peace Studies. The distinction between peacekeepers and peacemakers is thus becoming blurred.

I wish that the United Kingdom would follow the Scandinavian countries in making serious study of the possibilities of national non-violent defence. I know that Britain has a budget for conflict resolution work, but how is it being used? Compared with the money the government is prepared to spend on upgrading nuclear weapons of mass destruction the sum allocated to conflict resolution is miniscule. On the website of the Allied Special Forces Association I found this quotation:

> There is no glory in war,
> only death, destruction,
> shattered bodies and
> disturbed minds.

How do I justify the costs of our release?

In brief, I cannot justify the large expenditure (speculated in the newspapers as between £8 and £9 million) in comparison with other causes that the money could have been used for. However, the outlay did achieve the desired result – our release – and I am constantly thankful to those who brought this about. The action has also effectively disbanded the Swords of Righteousness Brigade of Mujahideen.

The same could not be said for the vast sums of money that were supposed to achieve the reconstruction of Iraq's infrastructure. Three years after the original assault there is still a stuttering electricity supply and a lack of other essential facilities. Of far greater importance has been the loss of young soldiers' lives and those of countless civilians – an expenditure which has not brought about peace and security for the peoples of Iraq.

What are my reflections on the work of the Christian Peacemaker Teams?

Although I have made some criticism that the CPT did not take enough account of the risk in going to the isolated Sunni mosque, I appreciated the reason for that trip. One newspaper misquoted me as saying that the proposal to make the visit had been ill-conceived. The idea of visiting the Sunni mosque was fine – it was the practice that was less than perfect, because the mosque was so isolated. This was the mosque at which Giuliana Sgrena had been kidnapped on 4 February 2004 (she was released on 4 March 2004). When you have too much time to brood you look for someone to blame. I did blame CPT but now commend the bravery of the CPT members who stayed in Baghdad during our captivity.

I have had access to some parts of the CPT apartment log and have come to appreciate all that the team were able to do in Iraq in the face of many frustrations. The CPT have notable achievements to their credit, for example in terms of their work with detainees and in helping to set up Muslim Peacemaker Teams. Our captivity provided an opportunity for CPT to explain their motives and achievements to a much wider public. They tell me that one of the most heartening parts of the kidnap was the tremendous outpouring of support from all around the world to the head office in Chicago and also to teams in the field.

During captivity I did have some problems with the CPT ethos, which is suited to North American openness rather than to my elderly British reserve. At check-in time I was not prepared to share my inner thoughts. Following my release, CPT was insistent that I would need trauma counselling. They sent me a book on trauma counselling and I threw it straight in the waste bin. In return I sent them a copy of chapter one of Jerome K. Jerome's *Three Men in a Boat* in which the author goes to the British Museum reading room to look up a cure for hay fever. He flicks over the pages of the medical text and discovers that he has the symptoms of each disease he comes to – everything from Ague to Zymosis (except housemaid's knee). I do not want to know what symptoms I should be suffering from. I will deal with trauma in my own way.

CPT policy is to be outside party politics and independent of governments. Once we were captured, the diplomatic instincts of the countries involved came into play and there was a vast effort to secure the release of the nationals of the three countries involved. The CPT office in Chicago were very wary of the involvement of the police and of Family Liaison Officers with my wife. They also had reservations about the efforts of the Foreign Office to secure our release. CPT principles had to be sacrificed.

As far as I am aware no ransom was paid – a CPT rule – but considerable military force was used in order to release us and I was flown out of Baghdad in military aircraft.

Have my views of peacemaking changed?

My belief in the centrality of peacemaking in religious belief and practice has not changed. I consider non-violence to be an essential part of the Good News that Christianity and other faiths have to offer. I believe any gospel to be deficient if it does not include both a call to confront evil and a call to resolve the resultant conflict without resort to armed force. The church has failed in its mission because it found itself allied to the 'powers that be' when the Roman Emperor Constantine became a Christian in the fourth century. From then onwards it has been deeply implicated in warfare.

I have always considered the doctrine of the Just War to be a pagan doctrine, and indeed its origins lie in Classical thinking which developed in times when battles were fought face to face. There is no justification for 'Just War' in the teaching of Jesus. To compound the problem, the church has sought to update the doctrine of the Just War to accommodate modern warfare, in which the 'enemy' is unseen as the pilot presses the bomb release, and more civilians are killed than combatants. There has even been an attempt to extend the doctrine to pre-emptive strikes like the war against Iraq. I agree with the late Bishop Carroll Dozier of Memphis that the Just War theory should be consigned to the same drawer as the Flat Earth Theory.

I believe that Christian thinkers should use their energies – their moral imaginations – to extend the application of non-violent solutions to modern conflicts. I have found most Christians to be ignorant of the successes of non-violence, for example the overthrow of the Marcos regime in the Philippines in 1986, while few Muslims appear to have heard of Abdul Ghaffar Khan, the Muslim equivalent of Gandhi. He worked with a large non-violent 'army' during the latter years of British rule in the Indian sub-continent.

In terms of peacemaking, there is emphasis in most faiths on personal peace – peace within. That is certainly an important part of peacemaking. Martin Luther King emphasises that one cannot be a peacemaker until all hatred has been eliminated from one's being. I believe that faith is not merely a personal matter but must affect all parts of life, political as well as personal. I believe that the American theologian Reinhold Niebuhr was not writing from a 'Jesus' standpoint in his influential works *Moral Man and Immoral Society* (1932) and *Nature and Destiny of Man* (1941). He was writing from a 'real world' standpoint, expressing the view that it is all very well having ideals but we have to come to a Christian position in the 'real world'. He was against the absolute pacifist position. He took the view that it was too idealistic and did not reckon sufficiently with the temptations of power and the pervasiveness of sin.

I consider a commitment to non-violence to be part of the call to be Christian. It is also a challenge to be found in all other faiths and is a rational path for the humanist, the agnostic or the total non-believer.

Concern for peace leads directly to a concern about the causes of conflict. Peace and justice walk hand in hand. Thus Pat and I have always been keen supporters of Christian Aid and, through them, of the Jubilee Debt Campaign, Trade Justice and the Fairtrade Foundation.

Within the peace movement there are allied campaigns to reduce arms trading, stop children being recruited as soldiers, expose the use of rape as an instrument of war and, now, the Movement for the Abolition of War. If we have effectively abolished war in Western Europe as a tool of diplomacy, why can we not abolish it throughout the world?

How do I feel about the men who held us captive?

I am still not clear what their motive was. Sometimes they talked as patriots who wanted to rid their soil of foreign troops and sometimes, in more mercenary terms, as seekers after financial gain. I certainly do not wish them any harm. Within the limits of our confinement they treated us with some degree of humanity. As I walk in the English country-side I have thought that it would be good to show Uncle how lovely our scenery is. I hope that Nephew's children have a chance to develop into rounded human beings. Perhaps Junior will find a loving wife and Medicine Man will use his talents for the rebuilding rather than the destruction of his homeland.

Re-reading the last paragraph I realise how sloppily senti-mental it is! These men were members of an insurgent group responsible for the murder of Tom Fox. They all boasted of having been in action against Coalition forces and would have shot the rest of us if given the order. They held us in captivity in spite of pleas from all parts of the Muslim com-munity that such behaviour was un-Islamic. Perhaps we should have worked harder in an endeavour to teach them the ways of peace. However, if they are brought to justice I cannot see that a retributive punishment will serve any purpose and I am firmly against the death penalty.

How do I view the role of the media?

The media played a vital part in keeping our story before the public. On reflection I may have been too cautious on release in my reluctance to accept offers from the press, radio and television to tell my story. Jackie Shepherd, formerly of the Baptist Union, helped to fend off the many requests for interviews. I wished to recount my misadventure in my own way and to emphasise the Christian motives for going to Iraq rather than dwelling on the stories of capture and release; the dramatic events and the sordid details of daily life as a captive. There is also the fact that I become emotional when recalling some parts of the story. This was apparent when I was interviewed by Feargal Keane in BBC Radio 4's *Taking a Stand*. Although I consider the Feargal Keane interview went well – he gave me space to express my views – I am not very articulate and, as I age, recalling the words I want to use becomes harder. I fear that I did not perform well in the more aggressive BBC TV interview on *HARDtalk*.

I have been re-reading the press accounts of our release. I was surprised to learn that at the time of our release we were discovered blindfolded and tied up with our hands behind our backs. I also learned that we had been moved regularly from house to house to foil rescue bids; that the Canadians had received treatment in hospital on their release and that I had refused to fly home with the RAF. I discovered that I had been teaching medical ethics rather than physics during my university career. If I have the temerity to doubt the truth of these published 'facts' it is because I suffer the disadvantage of having been there.

In edited interviews with all media it is necessary to trust the editor. It has been my experience with the press that when you submit an account of an event the reporters or editors reject your wording and substitute their own. They omit the facts that you consider the most important in favour of their own emphasis on the story.

The wrath of General Sir Michael Jackson at my 'muted' thanks to the SAS does not surprise me since my view on the effectiveness of armed conflict is in direct opposition to his life's vocation. The newspapers, however, made this the major story after my release, thus following their maxim that bad news is better for circulation than good news.

In summary, I (and many so-called 'celebrities') want to use the media for my (our) purposes, and the media want to use me (us) for theirs!

I continue to be surprised that our captivity and release achieved such a great degree of public and media interest among so many other events concerning Iraq. For some, my story may represent an attempt to overcome the frustration at the failure of mass democratic action to change the mind of the government. At least, I was told that the Queen, on hearing of our release, had said that it was good to have some positive news for a change.

How has the experience affected my faith?

I have always had difficulties with the problem of evil. How can a God of compassion and mercy and love have created men and women so capable of forgetting compassion, mercy and love in their dealings with their fellow human beings? I accept that the Christian experience of a God who suffers with us provides a way into answering the problem. But there is so much suffering, and so many people who never have a chance either to enjoy the good gifts that God provides for us all in this world or to find the fulfilment that is every person's inheritance. This remains an unresolved dilemma and I continue to try to act in the faith that God is compassionate, merciful and loving.

'Is Baptist spirituality useful in such a situation?' My answer is 'no' – or largely 'no'. My problems with meditation have already been exposed. I find it difficult to concentrate and the contemporary Baptist forms of worship with their emphasis on songs of praise cannot be readily transferred to

conditions of confinement. The Quaker experience of still-
ness and the Roman Catholic tradition of contemplation
would be more applicable. Perhaps I should have joined the
Baptist Union Retreat Group that enjoys quieter approaches
to worship.

Shortly after my return to London I wrote to the
Squadron of the SAS based in Baghdad, thanking them for
releasing me. I reminded them that hundreds of thousands of
people were praying for our release, and that if God answers
prayer he does it through the agency of the intelligence
services and the SAS. Appended to my letter was a copy of
their badge – two wings (angels?) and a sword. I added a halo
to the badge. It is another irony that while the SAS are hardly
famous for their piety our captors were constant in prayer and
in the reading of the Qur'an.

Our church had to rediscover the discipline of praying
when hope seems almost lost. To the many people who see me

My sketch of the SAS logo with added halo

as the embodiment of answers to prayer I have to remind them that Tom Fox was the subject of as many prayers as I was.

The Muslim community joined with Christians and peoples of other faiths in writing appeals and in attending vigils. Links were made between the differing faiths. It is my hope that these links will be strengthened by mutual respect, understanding and eventually the acceptance that there are many paths through life. I have visited our local mosque on a number of occasions since my release to offer my thanks and to view their new building works. Further contacts between my church and the local Muslims have taken place.

From 6–9 July 2006 I was a guest at a major event in London, the Islam Expo at Alexandra Palace. I was invited to take part in the opening ceremony and joined in the two minutes' silence for the victims of the London transport bombings on 7 July 2005. At midday prayers that day a crowd of 1,000 worshippers listened to what I had to say. Later in the day I gave a prepared address at the official launch of the Cordoba Foundation for interfaith relationships, founded by Anas Altikriti, who had done so much to help the hostages. In November 2006 Anas came to speak to a gathering of Christians and Muslims at our church in Harrow.

I almost became a Muslim mascot (is there an oil sheikh with a gold model of me on the front of his Rolls Royce?) Perhaps I am a symbol of the compassionate side of the Muslim faith.

Did my trip to Iraq achieve anything worthwhile?

Although my trip failed in some of its modest aims (see chapter 2) there have been some positive results. Links have been forged between Muslims and Christians, and the worldwide fellowship of the Christian Church has been demonstrated – particularly in the support given to my wife and the extensive commitment to prayer for us.

Although my celebrity was achieved not by what I had done but rather by what was done to me, the high profile I have acquired has given me, and others, the opportunity to talk about non-violence and Christian peacemaking to new audiences.

I had hoped to meet Iraqi people and I reviewed my limited meetings in chapter 3 which describes our visits in Baghdad. Accounts of three of our meetings were typed into the CPT computer before I was taken into captivity and they detail some of the deprivations of the citizens of Baghdad.

Since my release I have met a number of Iraqis visiting England and I have tried to follow the situation through the media. I am writing this eight months after my release, and it is evident that the plight of the people has become far worse. There is increasing inter-communal violence, an increase in kidnapping and more murders of professional people. Professionals in particular are needed for the reconstruction of the country, but many are leaving to safeguard their families. It is common to hear Iraqi voices expressing their preference for life under the oppressive dictatorship of Saddam Hussein to the present anarchy.

Following an increase in tension between the Vatican and the Muslim world in the summer of 2006 I wanted reassurance that things were well with the Chaldean priest, Father Douglas. I discovered that his church had been bombed again in January 2006 following the publication in Denmark of cartoons showing the prophet. I was informed that Father Douglas had been wounded in the leg and moved to a slightly safer church in central Baghdad. In spite of the move, he was kidnapped in November 2006 and only released after nine days, having suffered physical abuse. Before that kidnapping, in October 2006 I sent him an email asking him if the St Mari Church was still functioning.

Here is the reply I received (with the spelling somewhat bettered):

Hi,
St Mari church use by a little people and they have a new priest there and many family run away 'cos they afraid about their kids and girls and themselves.

So terrible, so suffering, but we don't have hope for peace come again our country.

Italian Baptists celebrating my release

APPENDIX 1

The Appeal for My Release by Muslim Leaders

The full text of the letter published by the Muslim Association of Britain and signed by Muslim leaders from Lebanon (including Hezbollah), Iraq, Palestine (including Hamas), Malaysia, Kashmir, Saudi Arabia, Yemen, Bahrain, Pakistan, India, Jordan and Algeria.

We, the undersigned, call for the immediate release of the four Western peace activists who were kidnapped in Iraq last week. We have been saddened by the kidnapping of these peace activists whose only mission in Iraq has been to express solidarity with the Iraqi people and see for themselves the devastating effects of the US invasion of Iraq. They were intending to return home to inform the public opinion in their own countries about the destruction and havoc brought about by the invasion of Iraq by the United States of America and its allies.

We have come to learn that the Christian NGO to which these four activists belonged is a peace-loving organisation that is well-known for its support for the just causes of oppressed nations around the world and particular for its sympathy with the Palestinian and Iraqi peoples and its support for their struggle for emancipation from the shackles of occupation.

[197]

Such peace activists should have been welcomed into Iraq and treated as honourable guests instead of being kidnapped and used as a bargaining chip. Neither the hostages nor the organisation they represent possess the means of forcing the occupation authorities to free the Iraqis held in its detention centres across Iraq.

While fully supporting the right of the Iraqi people to resist occupation with all legitimate means, we denounce as illegitimate any act of aggression against innocent civilians irrespective of their religion or nationality. We therefore call for the immediate release of these four hostages and of all other Western civilians kidnapped in Iraq and urge whoever has the ability to play a role in the endeavour to secure their release and their safe return to their countries to spare no effort in this regard. All illegitimate acts of aggression against innocent civilians, including kidnappings, indiscriminate killing or other forms of harm inflicted upon non-combatants, only harm the just cause of the Iraqi people and their legitimate struggle for freedom and independence.

APPENDIX 2

My Tribute to Tom Fox

Read during Tom Fox's Memorial Service at Foundry United Methodist Church in Washington DC on 22 April 2006

I write as one of the three people who spent many weeks with Tom before he was taken from us and killed.

Rather more reserved than the rest of us, he forged a personal routine in captivity – from his two-minute bath and regular exercise to our daily worship, Bible study and 30 minutes of silence which he valued. He was upset when other events interfered with these spiritual exercises.

He accepted that my experience of CPT was limited as I could not join in the extensive discussions he had with Jim of CPT successes and failures; of its policies and planning. His loyalty to the CPT ethic of non-violence was outstanding.

He led worship in Quaker style and in Bible study followed the four exercises for each, not always accurately, recalled passage: first impressions, relevance to our life experience, difficulties in understanding and how the message would change our life. His contributions to these discussions were often profound and based on his extensive reading. It was like having René Girard present with us.

I remember Tom for his outstanding humanity. We often heard explosions in the city and he would pray for the victims and their families. He reminded us that our deprivations in captivity were paralleled by those in the lives of many in Iraq and the wider world. In captivity he volunteered to take on the greater discomforts.

In the many hours of talks together he gave us insights into his love of music, of the natural world and his family.

I salute Tom Fox.

London, England
April 2006

APPENDIX 3

Our Personal Statement of 8 December 2006

With Jim and Harmeet making our statement on 8 December 2006
(Odd Andersen/AFP/Getty Images)

This is the full text of the personal statement Jim, Harmeet and I released on 8 December 2006 in response to the request that we testify in a criminal trial in Iraq of four men alleged to have been our captors.

> We three, members of a Christian Peacemaker Teams (CPT) delegation to Iraq, were kidnapped on 26 November 2004 and held for 118 days before being freed by British and American forces

on 23 March 2006. Our friend and colleague, Tom Fox, an American citizen and full-time member of the CPT team working in Baghdad at the time, was kidnapped with us and murdered on 9 March 2006. We are immensely sad that he is not sitting with us here today.

On behalf of our families and CPT, we thank you for attending this press conference today. It was on this day a year ago that our captors threatened to execute us unless their demands were met. This ultimatum, unknown to us at the time, was a source of extreme distress for our families, friends and colleagues.

The deadline was extended by two days to 10 December, which is International Human Rights Day. On this day, people all over the world will commemorate the adoption of the Universal Declaration of Human Rights by the UN General Assembly in 1948 by speaking out for all those whose human dignity is being violated by torture, arbitrary imprisonment, poverty, racism, oppression or war.

We understand a number of men alleged to be our captors have been apprehended, charged with kidnapping, and are facing trial in the Central Criminal Court of Iraq. We have been asked by the police in our respective countries to testify in the trial. After much reflection upon our traditions, both Sikh and Christian, we are issuing this statement today.

We unconditionally forgive our captors for abducting and holding us. We have no desire to punish them. Punishment can never restore what was taken from us.

What our captors did was wrong. They caused us, our families and our friends great suffering. Yet we bear no malice towards them and have no wish for retribution. Should those who have been charged with holding us hostage be brought to trial and convicted, we ask that they be granted all possible leniency. We categorically lay aside any rights we may have over them.

In our view, the catastrophic levels of violence and the lack of effective protection of human rights in Iraq is inextricably linked to the US-led invasion and occupation. As for many others, the actions of our kidnappers were part of a cycle of violence they themselves experienced. While this is no way justifies what the men charged with our kidnapping are alleged to have done, we feel this must be considered in any potential judgment.

Forgiveness is an essential part of Sikh, Christian and Muslim teaching. Guru Nanak Dev Ji, the first of the Sikh Gurus said, '"Forgiveness" is my mother … ' and, 'Where there is forgiveness, there is God.' Jesus said, 'For if you forgive those who sin against you, your heavenly Father will also forgive you.' And of Prophet Muhammad (Peace Be Upon Him) it is told that once, while preaching in the city of Ta'if, he was abused, stoned and driven out of the city. An angel appeared to him and offered to crush the city between the two surrounding mountains if he ordered him to do so, whereupon the prophet (or Muhammad PBUH) said, 'No. Maybe from them or their offspring will come good deeds.'

Through the power of forgiveness, it is our hope that good deeds will come from the lives of our captors, and that we will all learn to reject the use of violence. We believe those who use violence against others are themselves harmed by the use of violence.

Kidnapping is a capital offence in Iraq and we understand that some of our captors could be sentenced to death. The death penalty is an irrevocable judgment. It erases all possibility that those who have harmed others, even seriously, can yet turn to good. We categorically oppose the death penalty.

By this commitment to forgiveness, we hope to plant a seed that one day will bear the fruits of healing and reconciliation for us, our captors, the peoples of Canada, New Zealand, the United Kingdom, the United States, and most of all, Iraq. We look forward to the day when the Universal Declaration of Human Rights is respected by all the world's people.

HARMEET SINGH SOODEN
NORMAN KEMBER
JAMES LONEY

Harmeet's drawing of the rose for Pat